Bear Attacks, Dog Teams and a Sinking Boat

And Other Life Lessons

MIKE SLOAN

Gary and I just below the north
peak of Denali 1971, 19,470 feet

ISBN 978-1-64468-379-8 (Paperback)
ISBN 978-1-64468-380-4 (Hardcover)
ISBN 978-1-64468-381-1 (Digital)

Covenant Books, Inc.
11661 Hwy 707
Murrells Inlet, SC 29576
www.covenantbooks.com

CONTENTS

1

Lesson from a Sinking Fishing Boat in Alaska

Bristol Bay—1982

A modern-day Jonah story.

Having been a logger for over twelve years, I had a chance to go fishing on a gill net boat in Bristol Bay, Alaska. I was ready for the new challenge and big money you make that I had always heard about. Never having been on a fishing boat and never spent days in a small boat out at sea, I was ignorant of what it all entails when you say, "Sure! I'll be your crew." Ignorance is not bliss in some things we do. I was always up for new adventure, especially making lots of money, but little did I know this would be a trip that would have me terrified and crying out to a God I didn't know. As they say "no atheist in a foxhole." Or in my case, even a logger can be saved when sinking on a boat in the middle of Bristol Bay. I found out God can use a storm and start engines, even if they are underwater.

The fishery in Bristol Bay is different than other fisheries as you cannot have a boat over thirty-two feet long, and that means living in a small space the size of a normal bathroom. In the beginning of the season, it is usually a crew of two—the skipper in my case was the guy who owned the boat and the permit and one deckhand, me, who was low man on every totem pole available, the grunt or fish picker. You are in Bristol bay for one reason—to fish, not to sleep, just to find and catch fish. You are not paid by the hour; you get a percentage of the total catch that is sold. If you catch a lot, you make a lot. If you don't catch much, you don't make much. You will work long hours, have little sleep, work hard, and be used to being ground to the bone. You have to get your share of the fish quota quick before others do. You fish as hard not catching fish as when you are—setting the nets and bringing them back in hours later, with fish or without. It is a total dictatorship form of government on the boat; the skipper is the only authority and the deckhand who is the guy being told what to do and when to do it. As a thirty-year-old logger, it was hard to be told to unwrap the skipper's candy bar. I hated cooking, and here, I was the cook. While he rested, I cooked and did dishes. You would be out for days at a time, always rocking, always big swells, always checking nets, always walking like a drunken sailor, and the seasickness was fun. I never got seasick until I went to shore and was in a grocery store and the shelves started moving up and down. I had to rush back to the boat as I was too used to the movement and my middle ear was also, even on land. Maybe logging wasn't so bad after all, and maybe I didn't want a career change after all.

You have to use gill nets, and that is drift net fishing. A *gill net* is a wall of *netting* that hangs vertically. With floats on top of the net and weights on the bottom of the net, it hangs like a ten-foot curtain in the water. Mesh sizes are designed to allow fish to get only their head through the *netting* but not their body. The fish's *gills* then get caught in the mesh as the fish tries to back out of the *net*. The boat has a big drum that will wind up the net full of fish. The deckhand must get the fish out of the net quickly as it comes over the stern and before it winds onto the big drum.

God provides a storm

The worst fear you have is the boat sinking out there. The water is forty degrees, and you won't last five minutes. You want to avoid the storms, and so everyone is always listening to the weather reports. These are small thirty-two-foot boats, and in a big storm, you're in over your head quick. When a storm with high winds and big waves are forecasted, all the sensible boats run into a place of shelter and wait it out. Most do, but most didn't have my skipper. He wanted to get fish and decided to stay out and ride a storm out. We are setting the nets when all the fury of the sea broke loose. As the swells became bigger than the boat, we realized we were in trouble and had to get back to shelter, which was usually a three-hour run to land. You might find a slow-moving river coming out of the tundra, which would give you a safe place to anchor. We stumbled and crawled to the back of the boat to get the nets in to get out of there. I was on the back deck getting the fish out of the net when the skipper yells, "Hang on!" On a roller-coaster ride, that is fun to hear, but on a boat out in the Bering Sea, it is not a good thing to hear. I looked back, and all I could see was a wall of water ten feet curling over me and the boat. I braced myself, and the water hit, smashing me to the deck, ripping the nets off the drum, which meant we had no drag to keep the boat straight into the waves, so we immediately turned broadside into the giant waves. The door to the cabin was flying open, and the wave went through the door and into the engine area. The engine became submerged and quit. Now we had no power, no pumps, no drag, and we're almost rolling over in the big swells. When I stood up, I was knee-deep in cold water. I made my way to the wheelhouse where the captain was frantically trying to start the engine, which would not start. His eyes said it all. We were doomed. *His eyes had the same look you would get from passengers on an airplane over the Pacific Ocean at thirty thousand feet when the captain comes on and says, "We have lost both engines, and if you never paid attention to how to put your life jacket on, it's too late now.*" Looking out, all you could see were huge green waves trying to roll us over as we were helplessly hitting them broadside. No engine, no power, no pumps, no other boats around, and no hope. We were three hours from any safety, and I was up to my knees in cold water hanging on and trying to keep upright in the violent waves. I prayed to God. Now I had prayed before when in trouble usually when I was in high school, and it was things like, "Please let me get a D in that class instead of an F" or "Please let that girl I like not to notice my pimples." Standing knee-deep in water in a boat about to be rolled over, I prayed a desperate dying man's prayer. Make no mistake, we were going to die. Even the seasoned skipper was scared and knew we were soon dead as he was desperately trying to start an engine underwater.

God provides a whale.

As I was braced in the corner, I prayed, "God, if you get me out of this, I will do anything you want." Just as I finished praying, the engine started! We got the pumps going, and the boat positioned into the waves that were beating us. We were able to head to land and three hours later found a slough to go up and anchor for the night. I *realized that God provided a storm for me, and He provided a whale.*

God can still start an engine underwater.

The next day, as I laid in the bunk, I knew I was different. Something had changed. My thoughts were centered on God. The skipper had no explanation for the engine starting, but I knew who started it. When I got home, we started going to church, and I went back to logging. I worked with a Christian guy who was very instrumental in my early discipleship.

> Some went out on the sea in ships;
> they were merchants on the mighty waters.
> They saw the works of the Lord,
> his wonderful deeds in the deep.
> For he spoke and stirred up a tempest
> that lifted high the waves.

They mounted up to the heavens and went down
    to the depths;
in their peril their courage melted away.
They reeled and staggered like drunkards;
they were at their wits' end
Then they cried out to the Lord in their trouble,
and he brought them out of their distress.
He stilled the storm to a whisper;
the waves of the sea were hushed.
They were glad when it grew calm,
and he guided them to their desired haven.
Let them give thanks to the Lord for his unfailing
    love (Psalm 107:23–31)

That Psalm is my testimony. There is nothing like a storm at sea to humble a person. I know God saved us, and only He could have started that engine. You see, God still does miracles in reaching down to us. He can use a storm that will bring you to Him. He can even start an engine underwater. You may not need a submerged engine to start, but God knows exactly what you do need. Just ask.

Lesson from a Football Game

Learn to spot the peanut sellers.

A football game is a great analogy. You have eleven people on the field playing, doing the work. You have many others on the team in the player's area who play also. These people are all in and committed to the game. The coaches are the ones to come up with plans, watch the game, call out different plays, and if they win get ice dumped on them. The team is who everyone is watching, and whether they play every play perfect or not, the game still goes on. If the team wins or loses, it will be there on the field. It will depend on the players doing their best in their different positions. Each team could have the best coach, but if the receivers can't catch and the blockers don't block, the best coach in the world won't matter.

There are the team's cheerleaders who are responsible to keep the fan excitement going. Their energy and excitement are passed on to the fans. Hopefully, they are encouraging their team too.

Then you have the fans in the stadium who are cheering their team on. They often wear the team clothing and colors. I'm always amazed when I fly into Seattle at the number of people with Seahawks shirts, hats, and other articles of clothing on and if they are not taking their medicine for the day, even painting their faces. A disclaimer here—I'm not a football fan. I've never cared for the sport. The fans of the team are everywhere, not only in the stadium where the game is playing. Their support and investment in the team is vital even when there is not a game. My wife's dad was a doctor in Seattle and loved football. He had his favorite team, and he would follow the games through the whole season. The thing that amazed me was he could talk about every player on the team and list their strong and weak areas. He knew what they did in the season, how they performed, their running yards, throwing yards, etc. When Molly and I were first dating, naturally I wanted to make a good impression with this future father-in-law. When we would be around his house, he would usually resort to talking football, describing his favorite player to me, etc. I might as well be in my tenth-grade calculus class. It was total Greek to me. I did have the same open mouth, same bewildered look on my face, eyes glazing over and wondering how time itself can miraculously slow down at these particular times. He soon learned to spend his time with the other nine sons-in-law because they were football fans and could offer some kind of input that made sense. One thing is certain, the fans are an important part of the game and want their team to win, and even though they are not playing, they are invested in their team winning.

There is another group in the stadium whom I call the peanut sellers. They make money selling hot dogs, peanuts, and other items to the fans. Wandering up and down the aisles selling their items, they are taking advantage of the fans gathered. The thing about the peanut sellers are they aren't invested in the game. It doesn't matter who wins or loses, they still sell their items. Ultimately whether the team wins or loses, they don't care. They just need a crowd. As they cannot gather a crowd on their own, they have to have someone gather a crowd for them. When the crowd gathers at another place, they will have another opportunity for selling their items.

Being invested is crucial.

Having been in ministry and pastored for thirty-eight years, I see this as very similar to the church. You have the team, those doing the game, the staff, volunteers, teachers, worship people, media, sound, and secretaries. These are the ones in the field playing the game. They are the ones each day on the field sweating, tired, or excited as they are looking for their part in the next play.

Then you have the stadium full of the sold-out fans who are invested in the team. They support the team with their offerings and tithes and wear the colors of the team. They want the team to win and see their part as supporting the team in any way they can. Dedicated and invested, they show up and identify with their team.

You need to beware of the peanut sellers.

You have another part of the equation that I've seen and watched for which I call the peanut sellers. These are the people who cannot gather a crowd on their own but have their items to sell, so they need someone to gather a crowd for them. Their agenda is to sell their "items," usually their "pet doctrine," like an end-times focus or focus on a gift they feel they have. This needs a crowd. Basically, they are not there to serve in the game, the people in the stadium, or the church. They are there to be listened to and gain a following to affirm their identity, and they are looking for the filled stadiums or church gatherings. The problem is they don't care if a particular team wins or loses. They usually move on to another game with a gathered crowd soon. That is what makes them so dangerous. They will find some other place to impact and get themselves noticed and fringe people to take out of the game. Sadly, these peanut sellers are around, and you have to watch for them.

Seeking a title or a testimony?

Over the last thirty-eight years of ministry, I have seen the peanut sellers selling their particular items. They are looking for a title or a prominent position of importance. I remember visiting a church in the Chicago area that was pretty lively. A guy suddenly got up and proceeded to say, "God says, 'This time next year, the rapture will happen.'" And he proceeded to emphasize his prophecy to make people listen and validate himself by saying, "If this is not true by this time next year, you can stone me outside in the parking lot." This was in 1991. The church is still there, and I'm pretty sure he wasn't stoned as the social pressure in America tends to make stoning of false prophets not appreciated. Besides it's hard to get in the mood for a good stoning after a church potluck. There are always going to be people that use the gifts for wrong reasons, and some are just plain counterfeit. These people are divisive and confusing for people in the game and are always gravitating toward people that will be attracted to their message and ultimately cause division in the church.

Paul had the same problem in his day.

> This is a trustworthy saying. And I want you to stress these things, so that those who have trusted in God may be careful to devote themselves to doing what is good. These things are excellent and profitable for everyone.
>
> But avoid foolish controversies and genealogies and arguments and quarrels about the law, because these are unprofitable and useless. Warn a divisive person once, and then warn them a second time. After that, have nothing to do with them. You may be sure that such people are warped and sinful; they are self-condemned. (Titus 3:8–12 NIV)

Paul's Final Instructions

> And now I make one more appeal, my dear brothers and sisters. Watch out for people who cause divisions and upset people's faith by teaching things contrary to what you have been taught. Stay away from them. Such people are not serving Christ our Lord; they are serving their own personal interests. By smooth talk and glowing words they deceive innocent people. (Romans 16:17–18 NLT)

You can counterfeit the gifts, but you can't counterfeit the fruits. Look for the fruit in a person's life. Do they evidence humbleness? Are they divisive? Do they use scripture? Do they insinuate that you are the person who is "quenching the spirit"? How long have they been a Christian? How long have they been coming to this "stadium" or church? Why did they leave their last church? Are they committed to the team? How have they evidenced it? Do they volunteer for behind-the-scenes things like church cleaning, ushering, or other areas that aren't up front? Time and faithfulness have to be evidenced as fruit of a godly life. In short, are they building a testimony by serving the team or wanting a title to validate themselves? A serving heart can be seen as they will work without the attention as cheerfully as when in front with attention. A person who suddenly appears and seeks to do something up front or strives after being the center of attention is perhaps a peanut seller. Beware of those who are seeking a title before a testimony.

Lesson about the Dangerous Middle

On the Muldrow glacier—Denali 1971

In between the beginning and the end—the dangerous middle.

In 1971, I did something that changed my life. I was eighteen and loved to climb in the nearby cascades. I was invited and joined an expedition to climb the highest peak on the North American continent—Mount McKinley (now called Denali). At 20,320 feet, it poses a definite challenge and dangerous climb to all who attempt it. Our route took us up the little climbed north side. First, starting with thirty-mile expanse of tundra and rivers to cross to reach the mountain. Then up a ridge called Pioneer Ridge that required us to climb the north peak (19,470 feet) first, then over to the south summit (20,320 feet). This route was never climbed all the way to the south peak as carrying full loads over the north peak made it very physically demanding.

The Climb

It's going to be adventurous and fun. Starting in May with thirty miles of hiking in on the still frozen snow-covered Alaska tundra to reach the base of the mountain. Carrying one-hundred-pound packs crossing rivers and endless tundra. Then back on the Muldrow glacier for 15 miles. Jumping over open crevasses that are bottomless dark cracks, then reaching the upper Muldrow glacier, which puts us navigating the treacherous *great icefall* area with blocks of ice the size of houses hanging precariously, we will finally reach the ten thousand feet area on the Muldrow glacier, and a right turn takes us climbing up to the official Pioneer Ridge that will take us to the top of the north peak, which is 19,470 feet. Then down into the famous windy and dangerous 18,000 feet, the Denali pass, where we will have to camp for some days waiting for the weather to allow a summit day. If the wind does not blow our tent apart, we will attempt to summit Denali south peak, which is the highest peak and then down a different ridge called Karstens Ridge, which takes us down onto the twenty-mile-long Muldrow glacier, then down to the tundra and the twenty miles of mosquito heaven tundra, hoping we don't see the numerous grizzly bears in the park.

Waiting near the end for us is the dreaded one-mile Mckinley River crossing. This is the dangerous one-mile-wide braided Mckinley River raging and running full of water as it is now July. If we get across that successfully, which many haven't, we will reach the Denali National Park road, which we then will catch a ride to the railroad station at the park entrance. Then off via train to Anchorage and on the plane home. Sounds fun and climbable. We were all excited as we met several times in the leader's warm house in February to package a month supply of food and fuel to ship up to the bush pilot at Talkeetna, Alaska. The five of us were ready, willing and devoted to do this one-month new ascent of Denali. Ah! Sweet smell of fun and a thirty-plus-day adventure! What could possibly go wrong?

We Are Headed for the Dangerous Middle

The middle is always a battle for the heart and real testing. Always decisions to be made that affect the outcome of the climb. In short, the middle is where it really starts and ends. A successful climb or not a successful climb is decided here, not in the beginning. The middle is where character is tested, where your commitment is tested. In short, this is where Egypt can look good, after all the onions were good. Our middle found us struggling for the last two weeks with painful blisters on the feet, snow, ice wind, and lousy food—carrying eighty-pound packs all day, setting the tent on the knife-edge ridge where any misstep spelled a three thousand foot fall. The tent was often hit with winds so extreme we would just hope our bodies would keep it from being blown off the ridge. I knew all were having fun when with each gust of wind, their eyes would get so big, I thought they could fall out and wondered why they didn't. We were not in Kansas anymore. With this in mind, do we really want to spend two more weeks doing this? Do we want to go even higher where escape gets more difficult or may not even be possible? This is where climbs begin to breakdown and people quit or keep going. Only takes one decision to head back down. The dangerous middle is where it is easy to make the easy choice. It is where the heart is tested. In short, it's where you as a person, the real person, is shown.

> Brothers and sisters, I do not consider myself yet to have taken hold of it. But one thing I do: Forgetting what is behind and straining toward what is ahead, I press on toward the goal to win the prize for which God has called me heavenward in Christ Jesus. (Philippians 3:13–15 NIV)

15,000' on Pioneer Ridge—Denali 1971

The Christian life is like this climb. I used to be surprised at those who have been following Jesus for ten to fifteen years and then fall away into a former life that they so happily rejected when a new Christian. Ah! The beginning is so fun and unique! Now I am not surprised that they found themselves in the dangerous middle. It is where their heart is tested. In short, it's where they as a person, the real person, is shown.

Your character is revealed in the middle.

The most important character trait we can develop is perseverance. It gets us from the happy, idealistic, untested beginning through the middle and to the end. Character is built in us over time; it allows us to say no to things today, in the middle, and in the finishing years. That's a "well done" I want to hear. Building faith that lasts is about building character that can persevere to the end. To finish the Christian race well is decided not in the first year of becoming a Christian but in the middle.

The middle is where you have to decide—to press on or go back to Egypt? When the middle becomes hard, it's easy to remember what was behind and fall back into it as it is something we can be secure in, even if it is a previous lifestyle of slavery to an addiction that we were saved out of. Forget what was behind, look toward the journey, enjoy the new land, and most of all keep straining ahead—the top is worth it.

Lesson on Our Place in the Line

The Golden Staircase—1898—on the Chilkoot trail.

B eware of the "me only" syndrome.

Past, future? It doesn't matter because it's all about today. It's the tendency of having tunnel vision of the present.

Every generation tends to think history starts and ends with them. It's natural to view our time as the most prominent and important period in history, after all we are living it now and hence consumed in its demands. It's hard to relate to a time one hundred years ago.

It's the usual "all history begins with me" syndrome.

So many times I have heard a pastor boast that world revival would start with them and ripple out into the world that's never been seen before. Or a new young short-term missionary claim that their generation has the real zeal and passion never before seen on earth, and they are the extreme generation for God.

Both statements imply that they will do and display what two thousand years of Christianity failed to do. Oh really?

It's great to be excited about God, but what about in Hebrews?

> Women received back their dead, raised to life again. There were others who were tortured, refusing to be released so that they might gain an even better resurrection. Some faced jeers and flogging, and even chains and imprisonment. They were put to death by stoning; they were sawed in two; they were killed by the sword. They went about in sheepskins and goatskins, destitute, persecuted and mistreated—the world was not worthy of them. They wandered in deserts and mountains, living in caves and in holes in the ground. (Hebrews 11:35–38 NIV)

Generations before us were full of passion and zeal, and we are all part of this plan of God that builds His church through the ages; we are still affected by their testimony and faith.

How to connect our present time with the other times is important or to put in proper perspective, our time in the midst of thousands of years of other "times" or other generations and perhaps thousands of other "times" yet to come. We are just one link in a long chain. This brings one to humility at the prospect of their generation now has their turn to be part of Christ's plan that started long before and will continue after; we merely have our turn. But there are others to come after me, and I'm following others that went before. Only a person with tunnel vision ignores all before and all yet to come and thinks they have the faith not seen before on earth nor will be again.

We are in a long line of people who went before us and those who will come after us.

* * * * *

I have hiked the thirty-three-mile Chilkoot hike several times with the youth from our church. The original route began near Skagway, Alaska, and ended in Dawson City, Canada. They arrived by boat to Skagway and from there would walk over the pass into Canada. Once in Canada, they would build boats to float the Yukon River to Dawson City. This is the famous route gold miners took to get into the interior of the Yukon to find the gold. The golden stairway picture shows the long line of prospectors all heading up over the Chilkoot summit and into Canada. That's how I see the generations; we are in the long line, following those who went before, and there are those that will follow us.

The beautiful part about not seeing yourself as the center of church history and synonymous with the best move of God ever is that it also infers that old was just as crucial to Christ's plan and has even helped to build the church of today, and this past "group" had a part of what you have today. Also, you become aware that there are those coming, some not yet born, that will climb this trail. If that is true, then one can only have a sense of thankfulness, awe, and humbleness. It is God who calls forth the generations, and He uses each generation for His kingdom.

> Who has done this and carried it through,
> calling forth the generations from the beginning?
> I, the Lord—with the first of them
> and with the last—I am he. (Isaiah 41:4 NIV)

God is a generational God and sees the whole line. That line is called the church, and He is invested in each generation to do their part as all generations are interconnected by faith in Jesus. This faith keeps us moving together and ahead.

It's just not about you; you're here because of the generations that came before, and you are here now with this generation of people, and you have an opportunity to leave something for the generations who are following you. Someday every generation will come together with the Lamb at the top and thank Him for His calling out each generation, *and we will thank each other for a job well done in their time on earth.*

A Lesson about Two Bear Attacks

Grizzly tracks by the cabin

Always have your weapon ready.

I do a lot of hiking in the Alaska bush. I have a bush cabin that sits in the wilderness next to Denali National Park. I spend a lot of time hiking around the wilds of Alaska. The cabin is a six-mile hike through the brush and swamps on a handmade trail. I also guide trips in the summer with folks from the lower forty-eight states that want the real Alaska experience. All are new to the Alaska wilderness but are excited to see animals in the wild. The one animal I worry about are the bears. We have two types of bears—the black bear and the grizzly bear. Both are big and, if they charge, can bring fear into the most experienced outdoor person. However, the grizzly is a beast all to themselves. They can stand twelve feet tall. While out in the wilds of Alaska, you are no longer top of the food chain, the grizzly is.

There are two types of a bear charge—a bluff charge or an aggressive charge.

The situation you worry about is surprising a sow bear with cubs. If you do encounter a sow with cubs, you better back away slowly. Don't run! Both black or grizzly are deadly when they feel their cubs are threatened. It quickly becomes a doubtful survival as you are viewed as a threat. They instantly go into aggressive mode, and when they charge, they are pumped full adrenaline. It's like the WWII movies of tanks flying over the ground plowing down anything in their path, but in this case, you're the target. They are fast and can turn on a dime. Grizzlies' paws are enormous, and their long claws can move a wheelbarrow of dirt in one scoop as they search for a ground squirrel hiding in a den in a burrow. If you have no gun or any protective equipment and are attacked, all you can do is play dead and hope that they will tire of mauling you and batting you around like an insignificant toy. If the encounter is with a single bear, you need to stand your ground. I have been charged several times, but they have always been bluff charges. A bluff charge is when they charge to see your reaction and establish dominance. They are not sure what you are or if you pose a danger. They will often stop and stand on their two legs and check you out. If you stand your ground, they usually look then leave, hopefully. If you run, you will trigger a chase, and they will chase you because they feel dominant. So unless you have someone with you that cannot outrun you and you can leave behind, stand your ground and show your dominance.

A Tale of Two Bear Attack Stories

While walking in the wilderness, you never strap your rifle on your pack. Always have it in your hands like your life depends on it, because it does. My son was a marine. He and his new wife were hiking five miles back to their truck after a camping trip. It was late but still light. His wife was ahead about fifty feet, and he was behind. She turned around just in time to see a big black bear charging Daniel from behind. She screamed at Daniel who immediately turned around and saw this big black bear raging toward him at a full run. He had no choice but to stand his ground. He threw his pack off and tried to get his rifle off the pack. He was so full of adrenaline, he lost his fine motor skills and couldn't work the little straps with his out-of-control shaking hands. With his wife yelling, the bear charging, and Daniel's hands shaking, he probably remembered how I told him never to strap a rifle on a pack.

As Daniel was struggling with his rifle, Lena took her pistol and fired into the air several times. She felt Daniel was worth standing for. This caused the bear to stop in its charge. Daniel finally got his rifle off and fired several times around the bear. Finally, the bear left. It was an aggressive charge, and without his wife's quick reactions, it would have been a disaster for both of them. He never straps his rifle on his pack anymore.

Another thing not to do.

Never set your rifle against a tree and walk away without it. I knew of an older woman who had a bush cabin you had to fly into. A pilot who was a friend of ours flew her into the cabin. She was sixty-five years old and just had heart surgery; she was supposed to take a rest. She went to her peaceful cabin in the Alaska wilderness for solitude and a rest.

She went up in late spring and noticed bear sign around the cabin. She went outside, and while getting near the woodshed, a black bear came out from below the cabin and chased her. This was spring, and they were just coming out of hibernation. They are hungry, cranky, and aggressive. She ran to the woodshed and climbed up into the rafters where the bear could not reach her. Since she had foolishly left her rifle in the cabin, she had no options. She had no other choice but to wait until the bear left before she could climb down and risk going to the cabin. The bear waited for her three days! When the bear finally left, she got down and got to the cabin.

Two days later, she got her rifle and walked down to the lake for water. As she was approaching the lake, she set her rifle against a tree and continued to the lake. She got her water and turned around to see the same bear running toward her down the path. She only had one choice—run to the tree where her rifle was and beat the bear to it. She ran and beat the bear to the tree where the rifle was, but by now, the bear was only fifty feet away. She put a shell into the chamber and fired; it was a misfire and didn't work. By now, the bear is twenty feet and closing fast. She ejected that shell and loaded another into the chamber and fired.

The gun did fire the new shell (the bear by then was only ten feet away), and the bullet killed the bear, but as it died, it rolled onto her. The full weight of the bear pinned her to the ground. She finally freed herself and went back to the cabin to rest. She never puts her rifle against a tree anymore.

When in bear country, never strap a rifle on your pack and never set it against a tree, and if charged, stand your ground.

As Christians, we have an enemy. This enemy prowls around looking for an opportunity to attack us. He is watching for us to put our protection down so that we are vulnerable. He is looking for that moment when we think we have no enemy and we think we are safe. Until we leave this earth, we have an enemy that is on the charge. Usually it is not such a dramatic event. Usually we are drawn into previous temptations, into previous life habits, or away by others. How many Christians have disarmed themselves and become defenseless against the events that take them down? Funny how when we were going to Bible school, I started getting all these incredible job offers. Funny that when I quit drinking, I was having beers offered to me all the time.

> For though we walk in the flesh, we do
> not war according to the flesh (for the weapons
> of our warfare are not of the flesh, but mighty
> before God to the casting down of strongholds).
> (2 Corinthians 10:3–4, ASV)

The Word of God is our weapon. It gives us power to say no to worldly passions and the attacks of the enemy. It gives us the ability to stand our ground.

"It is written."

I am always intrigued by how Jesus was tempted by Satan. He was tempted in the use of power and authority. He was tempted in the revelation of his identity and divinity. His answer was always the same, "It is written." Jesus always beat the enemy's attacks with what is written in the word of God.

Jesus had a road to walk, and He would not take any shortcuts. He stood his ground on what was written and would not let the darkness take it away.

You want to stand in testing, trials, and warfare? Keep the word of God with you, in you, and use it. Don't lean on your own understandings. You know what is right or wrong. Stand firm. If you set it down, you will find yourself in an attack without your weapon.

Sometimes the enemy just charges, and we have to stand our ground, tempting us with old habits or old ways. Stand your ground. He will tempt us with little choices that will lead to bigger choices. Stand your ground.

> Submit yourselves, then, to God. Resist the
> devil, and he will flee from you. (James 4:7 NIV)

In life, you need to find something worth defending, and don't let the darkness take it. You have to learn how to stand and not let it be taken from you. Once you decide that Jesus is worth standing for, stand! Stand today, tomorrow, and until the end. It is written—you are a son or daughter. God has a place for you. It is written—Jesus died for you. It is written—you are part of a kingdom. It is written—you must stand your ground in Him.

When the enemy charges, stand your ground and claim what is written. To run means the enemy will chase you. You stand not on your strength but on Jesus's strength as He has defeated the enemy. It is written.

Lesson from Shoes

Our avalanche debris at Crystal Mountain

Wear the right shoes for the right purpose.

I have worn all kinds of shoes that fitted me for special work. When I was logging, I had caulk boots, which were rugged high leather boots that have hundreds of little spikes on the sole. These spikes will save your life. Many times, a logger will be walking on slippery logs to escape some loose log or stump from above that is flying downhill toward you. Have you ever heard the song "These boots are made for walking"? "These caulk boots are made for running" or walking on slippery logs. When your feet are fitted with these, you can improve the odds and hopefully have a longer life in logging while being able to log successfully.

I would log all summer, fall, and spring, but in the winters, the mountains became impossible to drive due to snow. Then I would go to work at a ski area called Crystal Mountain. Since I loved skiing, I got a winter job on the professional ski patrol. One of the jobs we did was avalanche control. After every snowstorm, we would go out with small hand charges of dynamite. We would leave early in the morning before the slopes opened, and in the dark, we would take off on skis or climb up with skis to the many snow chutes that would threaten the lower ski runs with avalanches. The job was to stand on top of the ridges and pull the fuse igniter, then throw the dynamite charge into the top of the chute with the explosion causing an avalanche so it would be safe for the skiers below later. A young man's dream job—using explosives, causing massive snow avalanches, high adrenaline action if your caught in an avalanche, and packing on your back enough dynamite charges to open the safe at Fort Knox.

Our duties also included first aid for injured skiers and tobogganing them down the hill to their loved ones. This meant sitting at the top of the ski lifts in the patrol hut waiting for that call for an injured skier somewhere on the ski run who needs help. When the call came, we would grab a toboggan, and off we skied to the accident scene. We had a first aid kit around our waist, and the toboggans were equipped for most broken bones. You had to be skilled in first aid as well as skiing and be able to handle a toboggan with an adult strapped in while bringing it down the steepest hills. Any slip or fall on your part could cause the toboggan to tumble and the injured person to suffer more injuries and further ruin their already ruined day. Sometimes the injuries were minor, a sprained ankle or knee. Other times, it was very serious, neck or back injury, a broken leg, which could be a straightforward break or a compound fracture of the biggest bone in the body, the femur. One time I was alone on top and got a call for an injured skier. He was skiing and hit a lift tower. Off I went, found him, and knew it was serious. I put a splint on his broken leg, strapped him into the toboggan, and I began the long descent to the bottom of the ski hill to the first aid building. I knew time was urgent as he had other injuries. I got him to the first aid room and told his group he immediately needed to go to the hospital forty miles away in Enumclaw, Washington. They rushed off with him, and I called ahead to the hospital to make sure they knew a badly injured skier was coming. He got there barely in time, and he had a ruptured spleen, a torn kidney, and a broken leg. He would have died if he hadn't gotten to the hospital when he did.

What made all this possible? The boots on my feet that allowed me to get into skis which took me into action to get the injured skier down. I couldn't have helped him with any other footwear. It was the shoes that fitted me for life-saving action. Only they could securely fit into the binding of the skis.

Neither the caulk boots nor ski boots can be worn for any other occasion. They fit you for the work they were intended to do. They wouldn't be any help to wear at a dance because they are not intended at all for the work of dancing. You would not wear caulk boots into a house with a wood floor as they would leave hundreds of small spike marks in the floor.

In Bible school, my footwear was dress shoes. When I went to church, it was dress shoes. Playing sports, a different shoe, hiking shoes are different, golfing is a different shoe, running track a different shoe. All these shoes have one thing in common—they fit the wearer for the activity they are doing. Fishing boots were made for standing in water or rain all day. Your feet will work best if you put on the right shoe for the right activities.

Climbing on snow and ice, you are fitted with a special footwear. You have crampons that allow you to climb on solid ice. Without them, you would not go far nor live long.

When we went to Nepal, my footwear changed—it changed to sandals and tennis shoes. Trekking in the hot monsoons meant always wet feet, so sandals made life easy. Almost every season of my life has different footwear that fitted me for a different activity. Probably yours also.

A Christian has different footwear, and it equips them for a specific work.

Therefore put on the full armor of God, so that when the day of evil comes, you may be able to stand your ground, and after you have done everything, to stand. Stand firm then, with the belt of truth buckled around your waist, with the breastplate of righteousness in place, and with *your feet fitted with the readiness that comes from the gospel of peace.* In addition to all this, take up the shield of faith, with which you can extinguish all the flaming arrows of the evil one. Take the helmet of salvation and the sword of the Spirit, which is the word of God. (Ephesians 6:13–17, italics mine)

How beautiful on the mountains are the feet of those who bring good news, who proclaim *peace*, who bring good tidings, who proclaim salvation, who say to Zion, "Your God reigns!" (Isaiah 52:7, italics mine)

Attaching crampons on Denali

We are fitted for the work of sharing the gospel of peace. Our feet are fitted with the ability to get us to places to share the message of peace. We are sent by God; we don't send ourselves. We proclaim His message. These shoes allow us to proclaim. They ready us for action, to announce that *you can have peace with God.*

> Peace—your captivity to sin is *over.*
> Peace—He has your best in mind.
> Peace—He has a plan for you.
> Peace—He is faithful to His plans.
> Peace—He is sovereign over the nations.

We have a special shoe that equips us for His work. Our old shoes won't work for His work. The soldier must have firm shoes to allow him to cover the ground. That's why the feet are beautiful who share the good news in this world.

> Wear shoes that are able to speed you on as you preach the Good News of peace with God. (Ephesians 6:15 TLB)

> And how can anyone preach unless they are sent? As it is written: "How beautiful are the feet of those who bring good news! (Romans 10:15 NIV)

Lesson from a Dog Team

Don't be the cause of a dog team fight.

Alaska is a unique place. We have lived here for twenty years. We get lots of snow for seven long months. It's a great place if you like winter sports or hobbies. One of the big interests up here is dog sledding or mushing. While driving to town, it's common to see mushers with their dogs alongside the road giving the dogs a run. From a distance, it looks pretty easy. Just stand on the sled and get pulled along on the snow. The reality is they are a highly trained team of excited, energetic dogs that live to pull and run. I know some mushers, and one time, we were allowed to take their team for a run. The rule is never let go of the sled as the dogs will keep going, and you'll be in trouble if you see your only way back disappearing over the mountain, especially if your snowshoes are on the sled neatly packed away and tied down. I got on a sled and held on looking at eight dogs' rear ends. Two dogs are fun and easy to control. When you have eight dogs, it's a powerhouse of excitement. I can't remember what I said, but they must have known they had a green horn on the back. When they took off, my head went back so hard I thought I got whiplash. My hands held on to the sled as if I was hanging on for dear life. Off they went with a jerk and quickly gained speed, a lot of speed. Up ahead was a sharp turn to the right, and no one ever told me about leaning with the sled, so as we hit the corner, it flipped over, and I just held on being dragged in the snow. I could have yelled stop, but my mouth was full of snow. I looked like a flag in the wind behind a rocket trying to keep hold of my only way back as they sped along barking. I finally got them to stop, righted the sled, and somehow got back to the cabin and the owner.

Eight sled dogs are a fast, powerful pulling machine team. Add the number of dogs they use on the Iditarod sled race to Nome, Alaska, to fourteen dogs, and you potentially have a nightmare of fighting, snarling, confused, angry, biting-at-everything, tearing into each other dogs, all of which are exasperated by their ever increasing tangled harnesses. The more they fight, the more entangled they become with each other as they are all interconnected with harnesses. They can't get away. If you're in the middle, you can get killed, hurt badly, or at least bitten a lot if you end up in this violent mess of dogs. This is what happened to my wife and I one quiet snowy morning on a walk in front of our house in Alaska.

Our driveway was long, joining the main road that goes to the small town of Talkeetna, Alaska. Along the road was a sled dog track that mushers use to run their dogs. We had lots of snow that year, and so the snow on each side of the narrow driveway was around five feet high. It was like a tunnel going out to join the road. One cold, crispy morning, my wife and I were walking out our driveway with our little dog who was the runt of the litter, about the size of a shoebox yet had a brain that was telling him he was the biggest, baddest dog ever. He would always immediately charge any dog to prove this and then find himself standing underneath the other dog doing what dogs do, sniff each other. As we were nearing the main road looking out the tunnel, suddenly a large sled dog appeared in our sight at the end of our driveway. Since any dog is fair game, our little dog took off to teach him a lesson. He took off at a full run, and by the time he got to that dog, he failed to realize there were twelve other dogs following, all harnessed together, all excited, and all surprised by this sudden intruder trying to show his toughness. He ended up in the middle of a running team of dogs. Immediate total confusion broke out. The musher tried to gain control but couldn't. We ran up to grab our dog out of the mess when the lead dog circled back. My wife was caught in the middle surrounded by tangled dogs. She was swept off her feet and on the ground underneath the dogs all fighting with each other, biting anything and everything. I ran up with the musher to start pulling dogs apart. The snow was turning red with blood from fourteen dogs biting each other in their confused frenzy. Into the middle, we went pulling dogs apart to find Molly. When pulling these powerful dogs apart, you always lift them off the ground by the harness because once you get their front feet off the ground, they are easier to control. I grabbed my dog and threw him away into the snowbank and then went to get Molly out from under them. The musher and I finally got the dogs settled down and separated and got Molly up, who surprisingly had no bites. She did say her life flashed before her, and the thought that this was how she would die—killed by a team of dogs in the snow of Alaska.

There are two unique characteristics of a dog team that make a team stronger or can make it weaker. Being interdependent on each other, they are harnessed into the bigger team to all do their part in pulling the sled. They are a team that will only work if they act as a team. On a sled team, you have the *lead dogs*, which are the most critical part of the team. Lead dogs set the pace and keep the team on the trail. They are the dogs that know to go right or left as the musher gives the commands. They also keep the other dogs in the team moving by their pulling the others. The *swing dogs* are directly behind the lead dogs. The swing dogs help steer the team around corners. As lead dogs make a turn, they help keep the other dogs following in an orderly line. The *team dogs* are the muscle of the team, pulling the sled and maintaining the speed. The *wheel dogs* are the two dogs closest to the sled. They are usually the dogs that are the largest because they are the first to take on the weight of the load being pulled, especially during starts and climbs. Wheel dogs need to be calmer as they are constantly hearing the slamming of the sled runners behind them. Then of course, the driver or musher who acts like they are all in control until a small dog with a bad attitude ends up in the middle of your team of dogs.

It is very similar to the church. We are interdependent on one another as a team, all doing our part to make things happen. We are all equipped with gifts to do our part on the team. To make it work well takes everyone doing their part. We are strong when we work together.

> There are different kinds of gifts, but the same Spirit distributes them. There are different kinds of service, but the same Lord. There are different kinds of working, but in all of them and in everyone it is the same God at work. Now to each one the manifestation of the Spirit is given for the common good. (1 Corinthians 12:4–7 NIV)

Like a dog team, we can make the team weaker by fighting or destroying one another. The problem is we are harnessed together whether you like it or not. Being so close makes it easy to see problems instead of solutions. Being so close, we can see each other's weakness instead of potential strengths. One solution we often choose is to unharness and go to another team but soon develop the same pattern because working on a team means working with people that are not perfect.

> If you bite and devour each other, watch out or you will be destroyed by each other.
> So I say, walk by the Spirit, and you will not gratify the desires of the flesh. (Galatians 5:15–16 NIV)

Maybe, just maybe, we are the weak one on the team. God did not demand our perfection when giving us gifts. God just wants us to be faithful to the team we are in. Whatever part you have, whatever gift you have, use it so the team can be successful. We have a musher that is in control—Jesus.

A Lesson from the Wrong Bathroom

Read the signs before you barge in.

When my youngest son was twelve years old, we started a father-son project; we made a goal to climb all the highest points of each of the fifty states. The highest points in the Midwest to the east coast states, outside of New York, Virginia, and Maine, required little or no hiking as you could drive to the top. We spent lots of time traveling on the roads in each state, frantically driving to each high point before gates closed or darkness set in. It was a logistical nightmare, but we saw the incredibly beautiful country; you just had to get off the main interstates.

One time when we were driving through Louisiana to complete Florida, Mississippi, and Louisiana, we passed a naval base that offered a museum and gift shop for visitors. Since I'd been drinking coffee all night, I was in panic mode for a stop. We pulled in, and I rushed into the empty gift store and into the bathroom. Perfect, there were no people in it; then, I noticed that there were only two stalls, and no urinals—oh well, this must be the way it is in Louisiana. While I was relaxing in one stall, suddenly the bathroom became crowded with ladies who were just getting off a tour bus! Two lines formed, one line for the one stall that did not have a panicked male hiding and a longer line for the stall where this panicked male, me, was hiding in. In my haste, I entered the women's bathroom; and I was in trouble, and there was no way out. Now I know what the Hunchback of Notre Dame felt like when he saw all the villagers coming for him with pitchforks and torches. As the line grew longer, as for some reason every bus in Louisiana had to stop here today, this minute, to use the bathrooms, soon these ladies became unhappy, and they started knocking, asking if I was okay, loudly saying, "There are other people out here!" I walked out, and they had the same look on their faces as if I was a Chinese factory manager saying their first-borns all had to go to China and make shoes for Walmart and the NBA. It was a humbling experience.

I should have read the signs before barging in.

I remember a missionary gave great advice to me. When you first get to the field, best thing to do is shut up, listen, and observe for a year before you start trying to fix everything. Good advice. In other words, learn to read the signs before barging in.

Ministry brings lots of opportunities for mistakes. We make it worse by not reading the signs before we barge in.

When you get to a new church or ministry, the most important thing you can do is build relationships; take some time to read the signs. Who are the ones that can be demanding? Who are the ones that are the foundation, the ones whom people look up to? Who are the chronic complainers? Who are those that need help and will appreciate it? Who are those who always are needing help but never appreciate it? They just expect more. Who is operating in gifts now?

How effective are they and how can they be better placed? Who are the overworked and how long do they have before they step down? How can they be given a rest? Who can step in and how can they be prepared? What are the areas cultural values? For instance, are they a hunting community. If so, don't plan church picnics on opening day of deer or elk season, or you will be by yourself looking in a mirror for company.

Before bringing all your ideas, take some time observing What does the community need and what are the special cultural differences from where you came from? For instance, if you came from a city into a rural community, there are differences. It's about how you can relate to the community culture around you, not how they can change to the previous community culture you're from.

Take time to read the signs before you barge in. It could save you some headaches and trouble.

> Let the wise listen and add to their learning,
> and let the discerning get guidance. (Proverbs 1:5
> NIV)

Lesson from a Skinny Kid

Beware of the five-day muscle-building programs.

When I got into high school, it was obvious, especially when I sat next to a guy on the football team. In my limited knowledge about God, I was sure he gave all the muscles away to everyone else and needed me to be a showcase of what life could have been like for them without muscles. A teenage guy is pretty self-aware and always comparing his miserable state of existence to others who seem to be in a better place to attract the girls. If I wore a short sleeve shirt, it looked like two broom handles with hands on the ends.

Then a miracle happened! It's one of those days when you're looking in the mirror and flexing, and you keep hitting yourself in the head with your clenched fist because you don't have enough muscle to do both lift and stop the arm. You see an ad in the comic book you're reading, and it has the headline, "Build Huge Muscles in 5 Days." You start to read, and it's got a picture of a bunch of high school boys and girls on a beach. A skinny guy is sitting with his glamorous girlfriend, and a big muscle-bound youth comes up and takes his girl. To add insult to injury, he kicks sand in his face and laughs. His former girlfriend is happily arm in arm walking off into the sunset with Mr. Sherman Tank on two legs. The guy who just lost the love of his life looks at his skinny arms and is hunched over in depression over, so his backbones are showing on his back. Could have been my twin outside of the few minutes he had that glamorous girlfriend. He is disappointed, and there is nothing he can do about it. Then the next story in the comic book showed him home reading a comic and seeing this add, "Build huge muscles in 5 days with our muscle building stuff." In the next clip, he sends away for it and gets it in the mail. After five days, it shows him walking on the beach with huge muscle-bound arms as big as a trash can. His legs look like two old growth redwood trees. Next clip, he sees his former girlfriend on the beach with the guy that took her, and he walks up and impresses the girl and takes her from him like a Viking on a wife-raiding party on the English coast in the eight hundreds. He kicks sand in the guy's face, and they go off happy and together.

So why not? I've got five days in my busy life schedule to get these muscles, so I sent away for this guaranteed five-day muscle building program. I can't wait for the new me.

Real muscle takes time and effort.

Needless to say, it was a total disappointment and didn't do anything. To build real muscle, it takes time, hard work, willing to sweat, and willing to hurt and be sore. There are no shortcuts.

Faith and the Five-Day Program

Faith building can be viewed the same way. A few lessons on faith, a few sermons, and there it is! Sorry, there are no "five-day faith-building programs." Faith is not built on a Sunday service. It's not even built by a Bible study. It requires us to step out of comfort zones where only God can act through us. Real faith takes more than a five-day program

The kind of faith I'm talking about is stepping out into the unknowns. It's launching into something that you have reason to be fearful about, or even go against people's advice to stay safe. It's a lifestyle, not a one-time deal. But you must start. God wants to build our faith in Him. It's his utmost promise and principle.

In April, 2015 I took a team to Nepal. All of the team were young guys, and they were excited. We got to the Bangkok airport and boarded the Thai airplane to Kathmandu. The plane had more than three hundred western tourists who were excited about exploring Nepal. We all boarded, and everyone was ready for adventure. Three hours later, the plane was starting the descent into the Kathmandu airport. All of a sudden, it pulled up and turned sharply south. The pilot came on and said Nepal just had a huge earthquake, and they couldn't land because the runway may be damaged. So we flew to Kolkata, India, got fuel, and went back to Bangkok. They gave us a hotel and told us they didn't know if they could fly tomorrow or not but would let us know.

Then the question to all on the plane was if flights are permitted, do you still want to go to Nepal? If not, refunds would be given by the airlines. I looked at the three young guys and one other guy with me and noticed their eyes hadn't blinked in twenty minutes, and their mouths were open. I looked at all the other western tourists saying no, and they will stay, as they want to live longer, and so they will enjoy Thailand.

You want to build faith or not? That was the question for us. I could easily have spent three weeks roaming Thailand with the team as I have been going there for thirty-five years. Nepal was in a disaster, fifteen thousand killed and my Nepali friends shaken. It was a disaster and dangerous due to the uncertainty of aftershocks. I told the team I wanted to go to Nepal and help. Nepal needs us more, and I can't guarantee anything but a stepping out together in real faith. It would be a dangerous time and require hard work and willingness to sweat, and we would have no idea what to expect, but we should be willing to, perhaps, be hurt and be in harm's way. It would cause them to lay their life down. They all said they wanted to return to Nepal the next day.

We got to the Thai airliner, and it was given the all clear to fly to Nepal. Our team of five were the only westerners that jumped back on. The rest of the tourists stayed in Thailand. We arrived to a chaotic scene. All the flights were cancelled the day of the earthquake, so thousands of tourists were stranded. They all slept out in the open because no one wanted to go back to hotels. Most hotels are on narrow streets, and if they collapse, people in the hotel as well as everyone in the street are buried. We gave out as much water as we had. I had told the team to buy as much water in the Bangkok airport transit lounge because I was not sure of the availability of water in Kathmandu.

The need for the survivors was food and tents. We pooled all our money and bought bags of rice and tents and, through the Nepali church, got them to needy people. I put out the call to all the previous people I had taken to Nepal and was able to raise almost $20,000, which went for food and shelters. Before the government of Nepal could get mobilized, before world aid groups could start their process, we were supplying food and tents through the Nepali church. These young guys were now the eyes to the outside world. Local news stations Skyped with them. They were amazed what God did do.

The building of faith requires me to look upward and not downward. Faith will be where I am unsure, but I know that God is sure and trustworthy. The kind of faith I'm talking about is there when you step out into unknowns, launch into something that you have reason to be fearful about, or even go against people's advice to stay safe. It's a lifestyle, not a one-time deal. But you must start. God wants to build our faith in Him. It's God's utmost priority and promise.

Want spiritual muscle? Step out of the safe life into the faith life; there is no easy five-day programs. It's all about exercising and growing stronger in our faith.

> Consider it pure joy, my brothers and sisters, whenever you face trials of many kinds, because you know that the testing of your faith produces perseverance. Let perseverance finish its work so that you may be mature and complete, not lacking anything. (James 1:2–4 NIV)

Lesson from Grandma

The "wow" or the *wow*!

The church loves to parade those with the most dramatic recent testimonies from the most sinful life as the genuine article of what Jesus can do. The more dramatic, the more people give attention, the more they are paraded. The "wow" is one thing, but I'll take the antiques any day for an encouragement and a model of the Christian life. I have seen many of the wow's fall away when the testing and temptations come because their faith is new and not built up. They were put on display too early, and some became addicted to the new attention instead of addicted to the long process of being faithful. Remember, perseverance cannot be given; it has to be shown over time. It is built by trials, testing, and staying faithful. Jesus did not save us for the big, short "wow." He saved us for the long pressing on in Him to the end, the long *wow*.

I remember many years ago in a church service where they brought in some Christian bodybuilders for a service. As they stood in front dressed in tank tops and shorts, grunting and flexing their muscles for Jesus, all the people who were overweight, out of shape, skinny, and plain normal were exhausted just thinking about walking to their cars. They gave testimonies that were as extreme as their biceps as they became red-faced, bending over iron rods and tearing phone books all while praising Jesus. The veins on one guy's face were about to explode in his praising God with his arm flexed so all could see his arm muscles popping out of his skin. I looked at their arms, looked at mine, and could only hope Jesus still loves skinny people.

On the other hand, I knew a quiet older lady who as a wife of an unsaved husband daily prayed for her husband's salvation for forty-five years of their marriage. He finally accepted Jesus at an older age and then was hit by a car two weeks later and killed. That is inspiring faith and very impacting in its quiet, her faithfulness, her dedication for her husband's salvation, her faith that Jesus can save him, and her persevering in her faith. She never stopped praying for him.

Which is more awe-striking? More reliable? A brand-new Christian saved out from the worst life with a six-month-old faith or a faith that is unwavering, that has survived the best and worst moments of history, the ups and downs of life, the rise and falls of movements, the births and deaths of powerful leaders and is still persevering in the faith? A faith that many view as antique and without a "wow."

I am always drawn to Hebrews 11 for examples of what a life of faith looks like.

The thing that strikes me is perseverance, not the "wow." In Hebrews 11:13, it says, "All these people were still living by faith when they died."

It wasn't the "wow." It was the antique that was the emphasis.

Want to draw people to a life of faith? Draw attention to the faithful, persevering antiques.

Perhaps our grandmother's testimony would be worth listening to.

Lesson from Canoeing
a River in the Dark

Beware of zeal without wisdom

> Enthusiasm without knowledge is not good;
> impatience will get you into trouble. (Proverbs
> 19:2 GNT)

In 1972, at twenty years old, I was a climber and loved the outdoors. At that time, I was not a kayaker nor canoeist. I knew nothing of rivers and how to navigate them safely, but it looked like an adventure. I was dating a twenty-year-old girl that would enjoy adventure.

We went to a movie that gave me a new, sudden passion. The movie was *Deliverance* starring Burt Reynolds and Jon Voight. It was about friends who wanted to canoe the Cahulawassee River before it was dammed and turned into a lake. These friends go on a canoeing trip down this river. What adventure! It looked so fun and easy watching these guys canoe the river. I was enthralled and got so excited, I went out and bought a river canoe the next day and waited for the weekend to go canoe our first river! It was our second date, and what could possibly go wrong?

I learned a lesson. Canoeing a river without skill can get you into trouble. Canoeing a river with zeal without wisdom will definitely get you in trouble. But canoeing a river in the dark will really, really get you killed. And you should probably be more careful on your second date.

It was summer and Friday. We had the canoe loaded on top of my car. We had our paddles and life jackets. Molly and I both worked at the famous outdoor store in Seattle called Recreational Equipment or REI. After work, Molly and I went to canoe a part of the Skykomish River flowing out of Stevens Pass in northern Washington State. It's a big river and has lots of turbulence, and some parts are very dangerous. But hey, if Burt Reynolds can do it and have fun, so can we. We drove along the river until we found a good place to start. It was getting late. I figured it would be a ten-mile-long float.

We found a place we could put the canoe into the river, and so we started out on our new adventure. Fun at first, like a continuous roller-coaster ride, as long as you missed the big rocks, didn't flip over, loose a paddle, or wrap it around a rock in the middle of the river. What a way to impress this girl. But never do on a second date something you may not live through to have a third date.

Zeal without wisdom can lead to trouble.

In the beginning, I was so excited but soon started to panic! It got dark, real dark, and we were now at the mercy of a wild, raging river and caught in a fast current. We were stuck with nowhere to pull out and get to the highway; besides, I didn't even bring a headlamp. Then Molly said, "I hear something." Holding on to the canoe, we realized the noise up ahead in the dark distance was the sound of big rapids ahead or falls. We couldn't see anymore, but the loud sound meant only one thing, something big is ahead in the dark. I was hoping it was not falls but couldn't tell. Good thing for the darkness as Molly couldn't see the look of terror on my face and my quivering lips, thinking, *At our age with so much life ahead of us, why end it tonight?* We were not even able to paddle around the rocks because we could not see them until we hit them. I always heard the saying, "Up a creek without a paddle." I never heard, "Down a creek in the dark."

Something to be said about acquiring knowledge and skill with zeal.

As new Christians, we tend to have a lot of zeal. The experience is lacking but will come. The body of Christ is unique in what I call the marriage between wisdom and zeal. Put the two together, and you have an incredible union. The younger Christians tend to have all kinds of zeal and energy. The world needs that. The church needs that. The older Christians tend to have lots of learned experiences and have learned a lot over the years. This is wisdom. The world needs that. The church needs that. But you need to put both together as young Christians don't have a lot of experiences, and older Christians tend to lose their zeal or energy. The church can marry both together and see great things accomplished. We need each other.

We did survive but never did that again. Surprisingly we had more dates, and we did get married. Shortly after that, I ended up working with the Canadian Olympic National Champion in white water one-man canoeing. He sought a job at REI so he could be near the rivers of Washington for practice and training. I had the zeal; he had the wisdom. He taught me how to canoe white water rivers and the basic paddle strokes. I learned river canoeing skill and, with the zeal and love of canoeing, canoed many rivers in Washington and even entered some river-racing competition in canoes.

In ministry, I did many father-son or father-daughter eight-day wilderness canoe trips as a way to build bonds and memories. I always laughed the first day out as the canoes always looked like they were on the submarine zigzag down the lake. The dad in the back would be barking orders to the front person like the drill sergeant at the first day of boot camp. Then the second day, I would teach them how to paddle and control the boat from the back. They had lots of zeal but no skill. They needed both zeal and wisdom. Then the adventure became fun for both.

The beauty about the church is a person is never too old to be valuable to the body as years have taught many lessons and a young person, or a new excited Christian, is a valuable asset and is needed for the new ideas and energy.

Bring zeal and wisdom together, and it's good for everyone, and you may survive for another day.

12

Lesson from a Rope and a Hope

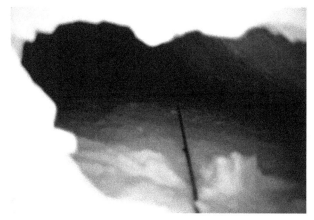

Looking into the dark—I'm at the end of the rope—1971

A tale of two climbers.

Nothing to simplify your life as when your whole existence depends on a rope and a hope.

In 1971, as I previously described, I was on a Denali expedition. After twenty-seven days of climbing, we finally made the summit. The next day after the summit day, we left our camp at eighteen thousand feet to begin our descent. We had been on the mountain twenty-eight days and are now heading out to civilization. We are descending the north side down an easier ridge called Karstens; we are trying to get back on to the Muldrow glacier and back to the igloo at ten thousand feet that we had built twenty-eight days before and stored our snowshoes, fuel, and food we needed for the way out. We had been descending for twenty hours from Denali pass the day after the summit day as we didn't want to set up a tent site and just wanted to get down to a lower altitude as we have been living on the upper mountain above eighteen thousand feet for seven days and needed to get lower as a member was not doing well in that altitude. We are tired of wind, below freezing temperatures, sleeping in a flapping tent all night on a knife-edged ridge, having to sleep with our boots in the sleeping bags so they didn't freeze at night, freeze-dried food, and homesick guys talking about their favorite food, and we were now getting in sight of the end of the trip. In short, we were like five schoolkids on the last day of school and wanted desperately to get to the beach with our friends. Now I know how it feels to win the one-hundred-million-dollar state lottery, and you can pick up the money in four days, but you have to swim the English Channel to claim it.

Your life on a climb depends on the little thin thing called the rope. This one hundred feet of lifeline ties climbers together, and if one falls, hopefully, he is saved by the other.

Your confidence on surviving a climbing fall is on one thing— hope. Hope your partner is skilled enough and capable to stop you. Otherwise, you both are dragged away together to an icy tomb.

Overconfidence and in a hurry—not good.

Finally, getting off the ridge and onto the level upper Muldrow glacier; this is a dynamic ever-changing glacier. The *Muldrow glacier* flows over thirty-two miles creating a maze of crisscrossing crevasses that we will have to navigate for twenty miles before we can go over a pass and walk the twenty miles of tundra to Wonder Lake. It's July 1 now, and at 4:00 a.m., it is still light, as at this time of year in Alaska, it is light all night. Immediately we started feeling better as staying for long periods over eighteen thousand feet, your body is basically dying due to lack of oxygen. Another thing that hit us was the warm weather. At at this altitude, it is warm, and for the last three weeks, the summer sun has turned the glacier into a wet, slushy walk onto a treacherous game of hidden crevasses covered by thin layers of snow.

Hidden crevasses happen when all winter they are covered with snow, and then in the summer, the snow melts but leaves a small, thin covering of snow over the crevasses that is not thick enough to support your weight. The usual careful way is prodding ahead of your steps with an ice axe. This is a slow process, and since we have been climbing for three weeks, defied death, sick of this, haven't showered in four weeks, all wanting to get out alive, we are in a hurry and over-confident. Gary and I have been leading on the entire climb. Gary and I on one rope, and the three others on their rope. Each day, Gary and I would start first to put the route in each day. Once the route was in, we would return to camp, and all begin the carry of food and fuel up to the next camp we established on the ridge we climbed. We were the youngest climbers and faster than the other three and usually one or two hours ahead. We were both young avid climbers. Gary was a former climbing guide on Mount Rainer, and I was in a mountain rescue group and an avid climber. We made a good climbing team. You have to totally trust the person your roped to as that is who can save your life.

A tale of two climbers—one survives and one dies.

After finally reaching the Muldrow glacier, it finally became a flat expanse of snow. While Gary was leading and sluggishly walking through the snow, he stopped. I came up to him, and we talked for a few minutes. The one hundred feet of rope that connects us is coiled on the snow. It is my turn to lead, so I start plowing through the slushy snow. I traveled about fifty feet, and suddenly without warning, I found myself in a free fall straight down. I fell into a hidden crevasse. Since Gary did not have a tight rope on me and the rope was just coiled on the snow, I freely dropped fifty feet before coming to the end of the rope tied to Gary. Gary happen to see me disappear and saw the rope that he is tied into flying into this hole faster than people going to a church potluck. Gary got into the self-arrest position to stop me, and when the rope tightened, the full force of my body weight along with the heavy pack on my back hit him full force from a free drop of fifty feet. I dragged him ten feet toward the dark hole as I was free falling into a bottomless dark chasm. One minute we were joking, and the next, I was spinning on a thin rope sixty feet down and hanging in midair in silence.

As you are hanging in a frozen dark crevasse, the first thing that strikes you is the silence, absolute silence, deafening silence.

The second thing that hits you is the dark void below you, absolute darkness, frightening darkness, lonely darkness.

The third thing that hits you is the coldness, a deep freeze of coldness, a penetrating coldness, an unmerciful coldness.

The fourth thing that hits you is a small white hole sixty feet above you where you fell through. Your rope runs up and through that hole to a guy named Gary who now is your only hope to help you get out. He is in a world of light, warmth, and safety. I am in a world of silence, coldness, death, and darkness with no way out but up.

The contrast is stark—you look down to a black bottomless chasm, that has death, and an icy tomb, and you look up to a small hole that has blue sky, life, and warmth.

The only thing saving me is a rope and hope. Gary sprang into action and, anchoring the rope I was on, freed himself to start helping me. He could not see me as it was too dark in the crevasse; he could not hear me as sound is insulated in those crevasses. He knew I was still alive as the rope was moving as I was struggling sixty feet below. He lowered me another rope with an ascender on it. With two ascenders, you can attach to your rope and use them to climb up your rope. They are a cam device with a sling for each foot. When you attach the cam device to the rope, put your foot in the sling and put weight on it; the cam device grips the rope to support your weight. With weight off, you can slide it up the rope. You can then slowly inch your way up the rope. With the other rope, I was able to attach it to my heavy pack and detach from it and get out of it so I could begin the slow ascent up the rope without the weight of my pack. After one hour, I reached the hole and out into the sun.

The first thing that hit me was the voice of Gary. I was in the land of the living. The second thing that hit me was the light and the sun. The third thing to hit me was the warmth of the sun. The fourth thing that hit me was the rope and the hope I had in Gary was well placed. Working together, I survived. Without the rope, I would have perished.

A few hours later, we arrived at our igloo we built twenty-nine days earlier where we left our snowshoes and food we needed for the way out.

The next day found us enjoying the sun and feasting on freeze-dried noodles for the hundredth time, and suddenly, we noticed a group of four climbers heading toward us. We haven't seen anyone else for four weeks, and we were excited to see some fresh faces. They stopped one hundred feet below us, and as we were watching, one person took off his rope and stepped out of his snowshoes. He took three steps and disappeared into a crevasse. They had a disaster and needed help. It suddenly became a rescue operation, so we went down there to help. Gary repelled down into the crevasse 150 feet and found his body wedged on a shelve. We rigged up a rescue system and pulled his body out.

Me coming out of the crevasse—1971

This guy died. I lived. What difference? He didn't have a rope, so he had no hope. I had a rope and had hope in my partner's ability to help save me. Therefore, he had no chance of survival as he fell into that deep, dark, cold crevasse. Didn't matter about the money he had, things he owned, family he had, if his cars ran, people that loved him; crevasses play no favorites to those who fall into them and only offer death, soon to join one of the many dead climbers in icy graves that this mountain holds on her glaciers. The only hope is to be roped with people that are skilled and that you can count on.

I had a hope because of a rope; he had no hope without a rope.

In the Christian life, we need a rope and a hope.

Looking into the dark abyss below me terrified and motivated me. Looking at light at the hole above gave me focus and energy

Those who hope in the Lord will renew their strength. When we become a Christian, Jesus is on the other end of our rope. He will never leave us nor forsake us. Keep your eyes on Jesus, the author and perfecter of our faith. He is the one that will save us. He will not fail us or let us drop. Keep your gaze up to the light, not down in the dark. It will motivate you to finish well. Jesus becomes my hope. I know He can save me. I know He will get me through this climb of life to join Him for eternity. I have to be roped in Him and put my hope in Him.

Those without Jesus have no hope or rope. Look at the life you had without Jesus and the dark abyss you were hanging over; it should motivate us and terrify us. Then look at Jesus and the light that should keep us focused on Him. Energy? It comes from our hope or knowing He will see me to the end and has the ability to not let me fall. After living in the light, why would you cut the rope and go back to the dark abyss?

Life is uncertain at best. The floor will fall out from beneath us all. I'm glad I got a rope and a hope.

> But they that hope in the Lord shall renew their strength, they shall take wings as eagles, they shall run and not be weary, they shall walk and not faint. (Isaiah 40:31 NIV)

13

Lesson from a Nepali T-Shirt

Trekking on the 1000 mile Great Himalaya Trail

You may be invisible, but you're not common.

Walking around the tourist section of Pokhara, Nepal, you will find lots of shops selling T-shirts. Some shirts are designed to attract the tourist who has completed one of the popular treks in Nepal. You see T-shirts with the popular Annapurna ten-day trek circuit outlined on the front with a map in bright lines and dots showing the various camps. There will also be Everest base camp T-shirts with big bright letters announcing Mount Everest outlined on it. Trekkers will buy them as a souvenir or memorial of what they've accomplished. They just want people to realize they were there and for their own recognition of what they did as important. Meanwhile, I walk around these streets in Nepal with a regular T-shirt that says…nothing. I just spent six years trekking and traveling the one-thousand-mile Great Himalayan Trail, hiking that mountain range from the western border to the eastern border. Alas, there was no T-shirt displaying this accomplishment, so I walk the streets of Pokhara and Kathmandu unnoticed compared to the ten-day Annapurna trekkers. I look like the common tourist on the streets of Nepal. My accomplishments are unknown to all I pass but known only to me. There are no T-shirts for what I've done.

It's natural for people to want to be noticed and their achievements to be recognized. Most of us want to feel like our lives counted for something important beyond the ordinary. As Christians, we look around and see people who are popular. Pastors are usually given recognition and have a following. Their position makes people strive to gain their attention. There are musicians and singers using their talent and skills to lead from the front. Their T-shirt has big bold letters that says "important leader," and their role obviously sets them apart. Meanwhile, there is that faithful teacher of the toddlers who has taught regularly for three years and no one notices. There is the missionary family that has said good-bye to family friends and moved into another culture. On their return home, they find themselves after a church service with people walking by thanking the pastor for such a great teaching. There are no T-shirts acknowledging their accomplishments.

Don't mistake being popular as being a validation from God of your ministry. Often popularity draws a temporary fan club that moves through a revolving door with the crowd seeking the next new leader. There is a difference between thinking you are just common to having the gift of invisibility.

Most are led to believe that they are ordinary and common and seek to find meaning through other's validation.

There is a need for encouragement, but the line becomes destructive when we seek validation from others. There is a difference between thinking I'm nothing special or I am just common to being invisible. The Billy Grahams are used to doing great works for the kingdom, but most kingdom work is done by those who are invisible. Most never speak before hundreds. They are just living life as a Jesus follower. But maybe, just maybe, being Billy Graham isn't the dream life. Maybe there's something equally significant, even preferable, about being the man or woman who lives in regular community with people, living side by side with them, celebrating births, dedicating babies, baptizing, marrying, burying the dead— really knowing and investing in people over the course of life. Maybe, just maybe, God is glorified by the unknowns of this world who are plodding through difficult ministry times. They may be at the end of their strength and yet continue on. They may look around and understand that they are invisible to most. This is what I call the gift of invisibility.

All Christians are living a super ordinary life in Christ. They are not just common but invisible to most but Christ.

You have an invisible T-shirt that says "super uncommon invisible important child of His kingdom." Just keep going. Keep running the race. Don't look to others for your significance, or you will find the crowd can be a hard task master.

Most of the time, we will never see the impact we have had. Every once in a while, we are given a reminder of what we do for Christ is not wasted. Last fall, I was in Nepal and ran into a Nepali Christian whom I know that was traveling in a remote area we were at six years earlier. At that time, we were five days back in the remote Himalayan mountains lost and trying to find a trail over a mountain range. We stopped for rice in a village. While eating, a village man came up to me and said he had an injured leg. I prayed for him and afterward gave him several tracts about Jesus. After eating, we started a long steep climb up a mountain to get in the next valley. Looking back down, I took a picture of the village as we climbed. I found out recently that after we left, he was healed! Others wanted to know what happened, and he just explained that we prayed in this God's name who was Jesus, and he was healed! Others came who were sick, and they prayed in Jesus's name, and they were also healed! All this was happening as we were trekking out trying to find our way out of the mountains. Reports are now that the whole village became Christian through this. All they had were the tracks and a windup cassette player I gave them with Jesus's teachings. A Nepali friend recently ran into one of the villagers who relayed the story to him, and he told me this last fall. I would never have known any of this, but the work we do is not common nor invisible.

* * * * *

You have a crowd of encouragers, but like you, they are unseen. Just keep going on the race Jesus has put you in. Your T-shirt is invisible to those around you, but it's not common to God.

> Therefore, since we are surrounded by such a great cloud of witnesses, let us throw off everything that hinders and the sin that so easily entangles. And let us run with perseverance the race marked out for us, fixing our eyes on Jesus, the pioneer and perfecter of faith. For the joy set before him he endured the cross, scorning its shame, and sat down at the right hand of the throne of God. Consider him who endured such opposition from sinners, so that you will not grow weary and lose heart. (Hebrews 12:1–3 NIV)

Lesson from a Puzzle

*G*od *can put the scattered pieces into a unique puzzle.*

God is patient. He works over time fitting all the pieces together to make His plans come together.

Galatians 4:4–5 says, "But when the set time had fully come, God sent his Son, born of a woman, born under the law, to redeem those under the law, that we might receive adoption to sonship."

Before the time had come to send His Son, a lot had to happen or many pieces of the puzzle had to come together to make the final big picture: a promise to Abraham, a nation gathered, a nation delivered from Egypt, a nation brought under the covenant of law, David's reign, the temple built, sacrifice system implemented, prophecy given about the coming messiah, Roman Empire in control, census ordered, Mary and Joseph travel to Bethlehem, the star shines for the birth, and finally the messiah would suffer to complete the scripture in Isaiah 53. I could go on with pages of examples.

Let's look at David—youngest shepherd boy of the family, proved an able warrior, had to flee from Saul, hid in the caves, anointed king, wants to build the temple but is forbidden, falls into adultery, has to flee Jerusalem when his son wants to overthrow him, David gives son responsibility to build temple, and David dies. Lots of scattered pieces, but what did God make of all of it?

Now when David had served God's purpose in his own generation, he fell asleep; he was buried with his ancestors and his body decayed. (Acts 13:36 NIV)

Do you think a God who does all that with Jesus first coming and with David will not put together the pieces in your life to make the complete plan happen? Nothing is wasted with God in your life.

All of my early life, I loved the outdoors. It was a place of refuge and challenge. The Boy Scouts, the camping trips, the hikes, I loved it. Later, during my senior year of high school, I started climbing mountains in the Washington Cascades. Not satisfied in flat places and the easy life, I was always looking up at the mountains and wanting to climb to the top.

Unknown to me, a scattered piece of my life was part of a future puzzle.

At eighteen years old, I joined a Mount McKinley expedition, an intense thirty-four-day climb of the highest peak in North America. We pioneered a hard route from the north side. We saw one death, and I almost died myself, but we were successful.

Another scattered piece.

Unknowing to me, this was another scattered piece of the puzzle that was going to come together in sixty years.

Then came marriage. We moved up into the woods north of Mount Rainier and built our first log cabin on a river. I started logging as a profession.

I got a job on a fishing boat in Alaska and in the midst of sinking, gave my life to God.

The puzzle is taking shape—all scattered pieces are part of a plan.

We went to Bible school to be missionaries and felt a call to Nepal. After three years of school, we were off to Nepal. We were put in a remote village with a small team for community development projects. Our village would take us three to four days of trekking to reach. It was a hard time because we didn't know the language, there was lots of sickness—in short, culture shock, falling into despair and wanting to go home. We stayed and survived as a family and were imprinted by the Nepali culture.

Pieces were coming together.

After almost four years in the village, we survived culture shock. We learned the basics of the language, could enjoy and cope with village living in the remote Himalayan mountains, and became accustomed to the intense trekking required living in those mountains. We came home and started working in churches and planted a church in Alaska where we now live.

A plan was coming together.

Several years ago, I started a project to walk the entire country of Nepal from the east to the west through the traversing the Himalayas. It's called the Great Himalayan Trail. It's about a thousand-mile trail through remote, hidden villages deep in the Himalayas. We would pass out tracks and show the Jesus movie in places that have never heard about the Christian faith.

It was then I realized how all the pieces came together to make this happen. God used my past love for the outdoors, the ability to hike and climb, the long hard process of learning the Nepali language and culture, and learning to trek in the Himalayan mountains. I would do eight- to ten-day treks seeing people and places tourist have never seen.

God's plan for us is like a puzzle. He puts the pieces together to make it all work. Sometimes that can take sixty years of life pieces, which are all an important part of the puzzle. It's the work He is preparing us for. If I was lacking any of those pieces, it would impact the puzzle. If I didn't stay in Nepal or didn't go at all, I would never be doing what I do today in that country. The puzzle would have been missing some essential pieces.

* * * * *

All the pieces of our lives can be used for His plan. What we need to do is have faith that God has a plan, stay faithful, and finish the race staying focused on Him.

He will bring the scattered pieces together completing a unique puzzle. It's called our life in Him. He knows how to put the pieces together to make a complete puzzle. What we think is scattered and unrelated is going to be used later to complete the puzzle of our life.

15

Lesson from Building a Log Cabin

Building our first log cabin—1976

Big things start with small steps.

I'm not sure when the desire of building a log cabin started, but since I can remember, that was my dream. That dream surfaced again when Molly and I got married, and we moved into the woods in the Cascade mountains to a small town called Greenwater, north of Mount Rainer. We decided to build one, and so we bought a lot in the trees and started clearing. We did things the hard way, dug the massive stumps out by hand, and built the foundation with river rock. I found some Alaska cedar snags at a ski hill area twenty miles away and got the forest service to sell them to me. Spent most of the summer cutting them down and getting them out so a logging truck could bring them down.

Problem is we don't realize the implications of small acts in the beginning and how they magnify in the future.

We were young, naïve, and energetic, what could possibly go wrong? The problem was I never built one before, and no one I knew had either. I found the book that shows how to build a log cabin and studied it as I had to learn how to make a notch, fit the logs, move logs and get them on the wall, select a ridge pole, and cut out doors and windows. I hand split cedar shakes for the roof. I was twenty-two, and Molly was twenty-one and from the city. We didn't know enough to count the cost before we started. But I was in my element and felt like Elvis Presley when he discovered a guitar and hair gel. It changed who we were. I loved it as we embraced the work, it changed us. We learned skills; working together, seeing it from start to finish, and building it with our own hands was rewarding. If you want to build a house fast, don't build with logs.

However, reality would set in, and it wasn't long until I realized this will be very slow and labor intensive. You would work all day to notch both ends and set one round of logs, which meant I had eight logs to set each time I wanted to gain one foot of height. Building a log house is different than a regular house—it is a lot more labor intensive. We did succeed and finally got a roof on it and moved it. It became our home for the next twelve years. It was doing little steps that other steps could be built on. You can't get things out of order in these steps. First, need to clear, build a foundation, set the house, and do the roof. No way to build if you get these steps out of order.

Most of the time in life, we are doing things we are comfortable doing, but there are times when we will do things we have never done before in life. Never been married before, never had kids before, never worried about retirement before, never taught Sunday school before, never worked with kids before, never traveled before, never worried about health before, etc. Life is full of new things. The fact is there we can grow as individuals when we do new things, regardless of the fact that we have never done it before. The best way to get somewhere is to start with little steps. Those steps open up potential future opportunities. Want to do something new, take a little step. God will always use our little steps.

The Israelites were always being put in a position to do new things to prepare them for the big thing. They had to leave Egypt, follow Moses, trust in God, and look to Him for all their needs. God always gave them little steps to take and would lead to building a bigger future. He was going to change this nation and would give small steps to do it. They really never understood that the little steps ahead lead to a greater future potential; also, little steps in the wrong directions would take away that future.

Jesus required the disciples in the New Testament to take steps. In fact, they had three years of taking steps with Jesus. Jesus had plans for them, and the little steps they took were about to become a huge future. Jesus was thorough and put lots of time into the building of their foundation to support what they were to do for the kingdom later, but it started with initial steps.

What Jesus is building you into is to be able to support something that he has prepared in advance for you. He is building you into a person that can support the work He will do with you. He is building you and will take all the time He needs. He knows it's a long process, lots of work, but you're worth it. Take those little steps that allow Him to make us into that big house called the people of God.

> For we are God's handiwork, created in Christ
> Jesus to do good works, which God prepared in
> advance for us to do. (Ephesians 2:10 NIV)

A Lesson from Death Valley

A sign located at Death Valley visitor center, an old advertisement

S *tay awake, really awake.*

We have heard of the frog in the slow boil illustration. Put a frog in water and slowly heat it up, and soon the frog will boil and not realize the temperature is getting beyond the limit of survival. It's probably true as I've seen it work with youth.

As my son and I had a project to climb the highest mountain of all fifty states, we drove to California to climb its high point, Mount

Whitney. At 14,505 feet above sea level, it is the tallest mountain in the lower forty-eight states or the second highest mountain of the fifty states. So off to Southern California to climb Whitney. It's a popular place, so your best bet is to get a one-day permit to climb. That means you have twenty-four hours to climb it; otherwise, you have to camp overnight, and that means getting an overnight permit by lottery, which is hard to get.

There were five of us, me and another dad with a daughter, another young girl, and Daniel, my son. We left the trail head at 11:00 p.m. in the dark to climb by headlamp. It would be a long day. It was a twenty-two-mile roundtrip climb, which would take fourteen to sixteen hours with a gain 6,800 feet in elevation. We climbed up in darkness for five hours until the sun started to rise. At 6:00 a.m., the view was awesome, and by 7:00 a.m., we were on the upper mountain and in snow. There was about six inches of new snow for the last two hours until we reached the summit. As we were leaving the summit and descending, the weather changed. It started snowing, and when we got lower, it turned into a cold rain. We were all exhausted, wet, and cold by the time we got back to the van. It was now about 1:00 p.m., and all of us piled into the van to drive down. Daniel and the other youth immediately grabbed an empty van seat for sleeping and being cold and wet, wrapped themselves in their fleece coats, and crawled into their sleeping bags. They quickly settled into a warm sleeping bag as they were cold, really cold.

As I started driving, I noticed we were not far from Death Valley, about 130 miles or two hours of driving. I headed there. We would go from the highest point in the lower forty-eight states to the lowest point. Death Valley, 282 feet below sea level, makes it the lowest point in the USA and makes it hot. I mean really hot. They were sleeping because they hadn't slept all night and had hiked for fourteen hours while I headed down in elevation. I noticed the outside temperatures were getting hotter as we entered the desert. To compensate and keep the youth comfortable, I switched from the van heater to the AC and kept the inside of the van cool. They never noticed the temperature change outside as inside was unchanged. They were comfortable, really comfortable.

I finally arrived at the visitor center at Death Valley. I pulled into the parking lot. There was no shade, only sun. It was hot, really hot. As I pulled to a stop and parked, there was a thermometer hanging for visitors to see. I parked in front of it, and it read 120 degrees. The van AC was keeping the inside cool, so no one woke up or realized how things had changed.

I turned the engine off, and we quietly shut the doors and ran for survival in the intense heat into the visitor center that had AC. We watched the van for activity.

In five minutes, the van came alive with activity, real activity. These climbing sleeping bags are tight, and when you're in a hurry to get out, it's not that easy. Zippers get stuck. It's even hard to get your arms out to free yourself. We could see hands and bodies shedding jackets. Clothes were flying around like a Walmart Black Friday sale. Shoes and socks were buried by now. The van became an oven that was cooking them. The door flew open, and out they came barefoot as they couldn't find shoes. Across the parking lot they came. The pavement was so hot their legs were going up and down like a sewing machine on full speed. They finally entered the visitor center and into the cool AC.

The problem with being comfortable. When you're hot or cold, you will be uncomfortable. If you're cold, you will awake and do something. It's uncomfortable. It makes you active. If you're hot, you're uncomfortable and will do something about it. When you're comfortable, you can get lazy and apathetic. The Bible calls it being lukewarm. In Revelation, it's an illustration.

> To the angel of the church in Laodicea write: These are the words of the Amen, the faithful and true witness, the ruler of God's creation. I know your deeds, that you are neither cold nor hot. I wish you were either one or the other! So, because you are lukewarm—neither hot nor cold—I am about to spit you out of my mouth. (Revelation 3:14–16 NIV)

In our spiritual journey, you need to keep awake, really awake. Don't let the slow process of becoming apathetic become a big problem. Being comfortable can become a liability in our growth in faith. Being hot or cold means we actively pursue God in desperate ways. It causes us to reach outside ourselves for a solution to being uncomfortable.

One thing that reveals we have become too comfortable in our Christian life is when we quit being thankful. Over time we take our life for granted. In fact, our lives consist of the daily normal and expected. Thankfulness keeps us acknowledging our dependency on God and appreciating God's hand in our lives daily, not just at Christmas.

I'm always surprised when people get a huge surprise gift of money or material things. They immediately praise God. I've heard things like, "We just got this large piece of beautiful land, and we are going to dedicate it to God." They then put up no trespassing sign and barbwire. Likewise, when in the hospital with some health problem, their thoughts and priorities are suddenly on God. I've heard things like, "If God gets me out of here, I'm going to get more involved in church." Often when they get out, they fall back into the old route. When life is going good, comfortable, and mundane, God gets taken for granted. Being thankful puts one's gaze of the soul onto something or someone outside of self. It keeps the person acknowledging their need and gratitude for another's input into their life. Funny how our thoughts turn to God in hot times as well as in the cold times. What about the comfortable times where most of our lives are lived? Don't let who you are today stop you from becoming who you could be tomorrow.

Before you get too comfortable and God starts to take a backseat in your life, remember where you came from, the cold days, and how that made you miserable and motivated you to do something about it. Also, be thankful, always thankful.

Lesson of Courage in the Himalaya Mountains of Nepal

One of the many Nepali bridges

Developing courage means being vulnerable.

Being vulnerable, remote, cut off from any security, no way to get out if sick or hurt, can be frightening or an adventure for others. The two ways we view risky activities—anxiety or withdrawal or adventure and embrace. Approaching things we fear or are nervous about has a certain level of risk that we are not used to.

I have been trekking in the Himalaya Mountains for twenty-five years now. I've been taking people from all over the world with me. It's always interesting to see the different reactions of young people as we trek further back into the remote, isolated areas of Nepal. It usually means some kind of problem will arise. Going into these hidden mountains can bring reactions as you become more detached from all you relied on. I've seen some start to become anxious and can't sleep. Each day is a day closer to getting out. Anxiety about losing their health is displayed as they quit eating the local rice and won't drink the tea, afraid they might get sick and die in this remote place; the rice is all there is to eat, and they get weaker. When you're eight days into the remote mountains of Nepal where the people have never seen westerners, you feel pretty vulnerable. Everyone has one thing in common. Building courage is often letting go of the things that give us security and launching into things that are risky.

In the remote Himalaya Mountains, you don't want problems because there are no roads, no 911, and no help around the corner. On one trip, we were four days into the mountains when a team member tried to jump over a small stream and landed wrong twisting his leg and tearing his meniscus. His kneecap was suddenly floating free and next to his Adam's apple. This is a big problem at a place that has absolutely no easy way out.

After the initial screaming, I gave him the five options. They were as follows:

1. Stay put until things heal.
2. Personally pay $10,000 dollars for Nepali military helicopter for rescue.
3. Limp out and handle the pain with every step.
4. We bury you here and have a great memorial service back home.
5. Hire four Nepali people to carry you out on a stretcher.

After my choices, he had the same shocked look as I do when I go to Walmart and get a shopping cart that actually goes straight. After a very short pause and thinking of loved ones at home, he picked number three. So we got a makeshift crutch, took his pack, and started the long journey out to the closest road to get a bus or jeep. His occasional scream kept us from jumping any streams on the way out. He got home, had an operation, and joined another trip one year later.

On another trip after a one day long hard descent, a person's hips gave out. There was no way he could go further. Fortunately, we were only a day out, so we hired four Nepalis to carry him back to the road on a stretcher. We continued on into the mountains. That was his first and last trek in Nepal.

The courage of Abraham:

> "The Lord had said to Abram, 'Go from your
> country, your people and your father's household
> to the land I will show you'" (Genesis 12:1 NIV).

Living in the remote back country of Nepal thirty years ago for four years has given me a new appreciation for what Abraham did and the courage he showed. We lived in a village called Nishi. It was not unusual to meet villagers who had never been more than a day from their village. They could not relate to other continents and traveling by air, so when they asked me where I came from, I could only respond in a way they could understand. I would say we lived many weeks away. They would be amazed as that is really far.

The other problem is tribal people are only safe when they are in their own area. Outside that area are people of another culture and language whom they have no ties with. At the entrance of the Nishi area on the trail, they would have an idol altar to the Nishi deity that protected them inside the Nishi village area. That deity guarded them from outside evil spirits. Outside that area was scary for them as they became vulnerable to the spirits of the other areas. Travel was not a safe thing to do. To take a long journey, they would get blessings from a shaman or Hindu priest, and he would tell them what day they could safely travel.

One can only imagine how much more dangerous it was for a person in Abraham's day to safely travel. Other people owned the land you're traveling through, and travelers would be viewed suspiciously as people just didn't take trips. Bandits, robbers, suspicious land owners, kings of other lands would view you as a raider. Other armies hearing about a new traveler would be watching. Money could always be made by capturing people and selling them into slavery to some passing caravan. Leaving family ties and moving to a new place was not safe. It put the whole family at risk. Without tribal alliances, you're completely vulnerable, and everyone knows it. Abraham had an incredible faith believing God was worth following, and he could trust Him. In short, Abraham had immense courage and faith. It made him a courageous follower of God.

How do you develop courage in people? The psychology and philosophical studies show that you can react to new unknowns or risky challenges in two ways. You can voluntarily react with an attitude of approach and challenge, which is what people do in extreme sports like climbing dangerous mountains. The risk is there, but it is viewed as a challenge thereby causing excitement, growth, and a pleasurable experience through achieving the goal. The other way is to act with defensive aggression or withdrawal, which will lead to anxieties and fear. This means any risk brings anxiety, withdrawal, and basically a negative emotion that is not rewarding but negative to us and our emotional state. The best approach for growth is to view new adventure and risky things as a challenge. This will be easier, and you will become more accepting of the adventures in our life that make us stronger and more courageous. Aggressive withdrawal will cause us worry, anxiety, and turmoil. It causes us to avoid new risky challenges by withdrawal and no growth. We can get insomnia, fears, panic attacks, etc. This becomes a partnership in our spiritual development as Christians. Accepting risky things in faith is key to developing courage with strong faith in God. It will not come by seeking comfort, and it will not come if we are not willing to take risks. Ultimately, we have to trust Jesus with our life as we step out in risky new situations where we are not comfortable or in control. It doesn't mean there are no risks. It's just that you see the risks as a way to develop a bolder faith. You trust that Jesus is with you even if you're not at your church on a Sunday. He can protect you "out there," and you become courageous as you see Him above your fears and anxiety and step into the unknowns.

Taking people into the Nepal mountains challenges their psyche and their realities developing their inward strength. The courage to accomplish the risks and survive will lead to developing bigger steps of courage in faith. Courageous people develop courage by taking little steps that build their confidence in their ability to see the positive in risk versus the negative. Courageous people cause others to be courageous.

The church needs to be developing courage in people. It's a process of growing. Faith being developed in partnership with courage is dynamic, and the kingdom of God is looking for the Abrahams who have courage to let go and face the unknowns for the kingdom. You will never develop that in a classroom or Bible study.

Lesson in Clothes

The right clothes at -30 F on top of the North
Peak of Denali 19,470'—1971. The 20,320'
Denali South peak 2 miles behind me

Beware of the wrong clothes.

Clothes help equip us for a specific purpose.

You would never show up to do a twenty-mile run in June in Arizona dressed for a cold -20 Alaska winter day. The heavy boots, gloves, face covering, wool hat, thick heavy coat, wind pants, with long underwear wouldn't get you very far in the race. If your purpose is to finish the race, you will dress in a way to give you a better advantage. Clothes help us do our job. A policeman or policewoman get your attention and their authority by their uniform. If someone walked up to your car after stopping you in a clown costume, you would think differently than a person in a uniform and badge.

A construction worker has clothes that help them work. A stockbroker wears clothes that help him identify with others in the same work they do. A logger has clothes that help perform work in the woods. A logger would never show up dressed as a banker or a sunbather on a California beach.

A climber's survival depends on the clothes they wear, especially on expeditions. You cannot cut back on the quality of the cold weather clothing.

Clothes define our group identity.

I grew up in the sixties. The clothing was unique and defined you. The hippie movement was going, and the clothes worn were an obvious identity to that hippie culture. You could see films of hippies all over Europe sitting in parks singing, and their clothes would look exactly like the clothing of hippies in Seattle sitting in parks singing were wearing.

Everyone uses clothes for an identity. For a youth, what you wear can make you cool or not cool. It will help you fit into your crowd. If you want to destroy lives of a teen, make them wear what the older generation wore in school. Each generation displays their own fashion that gives them a group identity. A teenager's existence is dependent on having the identity of their group by what their group wears. It would have been so much easier to go to a school that had uniforms, no choice each day. As you get older, your clothes can identify your work or what you do. Clothes help us fit into a group and show which group we are in. As you sit in an airport, you can see all the different airline employees wearing a distinct uniform that shows you which group or airlines they work for.

I remember when my son was graduating from high school and had enlisted in the marines. At the graduation ceremony, they had all the students who enlisted come up and were greeted by a representative of the military branch they were going into. They were presented with a scholarship award. The navy was represented as well as the Air

Force, Coast Guard, Army, Navy and the Marines. After each came up and was greeted by the recruiter, there was the applause. I was shocked as when those joining the marines were called up and the marine recruiter came out, a louder, more dramatic applause broke out. There was something about the marine uniform and what it represented. No one knew the recruiter; it was about the uniform and the uniqueness of the group identity. In this case, it wasn't the recruiter; it was the identity of the marine corps.

Clothes display our values.

Clothes identify us to a past value. Boy Scouts and Girl Scout uniforms represent the values of the organization. Likewise, if you saw a Nazi uniform, it would reflect the values of the holocaust and the terror that was inflicted on the human race. Clothes always represent a value behind the clothes. If you go to a hospital, nurses and doctors have their uniforms that bring security as their nurse outfit shows that they are representing your best interest as their value is helping people in times of sickness or accidents. You would not get the same sense of value if you entered the hospital and your doctor was dressed like Elvis doing shows in Vegas; he had a glittery shirt halfway open, gray chest hair showing, rings on every finger, and tight white-glittered bell bottom pants staring at you through sunglasses with diamonds on the frames looking down at you all the while pretending he is strumming a guitar. This would send the wrong value for you and not give you much security for this time of need. You want the doctor that is dressed like a doctor, whose clothes represent the values of a medical practitioner.

As a Christian, we have a new set of clothes. These clothes equip us for a specific purpose.

Clothed to equip us for His work.

> I am going to send you what my Father has promised; but stay in the city until you have been clothed with power from on high. (Luke 24:49 NIV)

We are clothed with a new set of clothes that allow us to do His work in the kingdom. We can do things we could never do before because of this new set of clothes. We are freed from past vices, walk in peace instead of shame, reveal the *author* of our faith, have joy instead of sorrow, and experience freedom instead of bondage. We are equipped to set coming generations free from generational sin that has followed us in generational lines. Now that is a great set of clothes that equip us for a great work.

> Rather, clothe yourselves with the Lord Jesus Christ, and do not think about how to grat-ify the desires of the flesh. (Romans 13:14 NIV)

We are clothed with Christ, and it reveals our group identity.

> For all of you who were baptized into Christ have clothed yourselves with Christ. (Galatians 3:27 NIV)

The body of Christ is unique; it is a single universal group called the church. Entering this group is only possible by being clothed in Him, baptized by the Holy Spirt into His family. No matter where you go in the world, His church is your identity, and all are part and all are clothed with Him.

Our new clothing should display the value of our group.

Our clothing represents values of what we represent. We are clothed with a value system that represents a kingdom. These values are distinct to our clothing and are revealed by our actions in life.

> Therefore, as God's chosen people, holy and dearly loved, clothe yourselves with compas-sion, kindness, humility, gentleness and patience. (Colossians 3:12 NIV)

Lesson from a Rifle Scope

Beware of the distance between what we expect and what we have.

When Daniel, my youngest son, turned eighteen, he went into the marines. He did three tours in Iraq and only got injured once. He also knew his weapons. When he got out of the marines, he moved back to Alaska. He got a job on the oil slopes in northern Alaska. He worked two weeks up there and then had two weeks off at home.

One time when he was on the slope working, he called to tell me he'd ordered a very expensive scope for his rifle. It was expensive, around $1,400, and was of top quality. He needed me to pick it up off his front porch as UPS would deliver it, and since he wasn't home, they would just set it on the porch. Since it was very expensive, he did not want to leave it there, so he asked me to pick it up for him. I'm always looking for ways to get revenge for all the diaper changes I did on him. I had an idea.

I went to Walmart, and there was a $5 plastic toy rifle with a bright orange fake scope. So I took the real scope out of the box and replaced it with the toy plastic one. I sealed up the box and waited for him to get home. I thought, he is a marine and will know immediately the fake scope, but it was worth a try.

He got home, and I took him the package. He eagerly opened the box to see this expensive scope he was expecting. He took out the orange plastic one, and he became speechless. First thing he said was, "Wow! It looked different in the catalog." Then he said, "It was supposed to be black." He proceeded to look through it. The plastic lenses were cloudy and didn't magnify anything. In fact, they had spilled over glue on the inside as a good measure to keep the toddlers from swallowing part of the scope. After all, this toy gun was for a six-year-old. They wouldn't know a scope from a bottle. I could tell he was totally stumped and was looking for adjustment dials and knobs. There weren't any, so I said, "This doesn't seem to be worth $1,400." It was all I could do to keep my composure but assured him this would be deadly if he could figure it out. I told him, "You got a great scope for that $1,400. You must not have the directions figured out." It was hard for him to accept it as he was excited and wanted to believe it was the real thing, and the alternative was crushing his excitement and plans. He was intensely inspecting the plastic toy scope to find the magic button that would make it what he was expecting. He had expectations of an incredible precision-built scope but instead got the reality of a scope that was totally not what he was expecting.

Sometimes the distance between our expectations and our reality are disappointing.

We have expectations in ministry. We have standards that should be achievable for people. After all, the standards Jesus laid out in His Word are absolute.

Ministry has its crucial make-or-break situations. You have your expectations in ministry, as we preach and teach a lot of challenging messages of these truths, desperately trying to help people better their lives and become more like Jesus. He is the real deal. Instead we get the plastic scope. You look for some knob to turn or teaching method to make it work. You preach serving others to amen and smiles only to find a lack of teachers for Sunday school. You teach on forgiveness for twenty-five years only to have people get offended over things like paint colors for a room. It's the reality of opening the box only to find the $5 scope.

The critical distance.

How you react is a make-or-break-it deal. How you deal with the apparent distance between where you want people to be in their walk with God and where they are? I have seen many get angry, critical, disappointed, and even quit and leave the church. I have seen some try to use rules and legalism to get people to reach "the standard." The dos and don'ts are fun to impose and seem to offer a surefire resolution, but that never works either. It sure manages to make a bunch of rebellious youth when they grow up and leave the rules of the church and house. I have seen some use guilt and shame as a spiritual spanking each Sunday from the pulpit. I have seen some water down the message to the level the people are at. That's a mistake because it starts to infiltrate our own lives. Our teaching should always be pulling people up, not revising my message to their level. Some devour the latest trend in church growth or newest big teacher by going to conferences and seminars in order to find the key. I have seen some think small groups are the answer, some think the gifts will cure the lack of spiritual growth. All are looking for a method to produce a genuine product but each Monday open the box to the reality—not enough volunteers, the worship leader is upset as the sound guy messed up, the lead singer is in a bad mood this morning, and, the icing on the cake, the bass player wants his mic moved up so people can see him. Where is that one button when you need it?

Good news! We are not responsible for the decisions people make, just responsible for our teaching and life example. Maybe we need to reevaluate our methods, maybe there are ways to be more effective. Maybe what we are currently doing is not effective. But bottom line is people are complex, and no one style of teaching, no one church structure has it figured out. It doesn't even matter if you have funny catchphrases for your sermon outlines.

How did Jesus handle the gap?

Where should His disciples be after three years of being with Him, seeing miracles, seeing healings, being taught, and seeing firsthand what Jesus is like? Where were they? One betrayal, all denied, scattered, hiding, afraid; Jesus was left alone, but he knew the future was still ahead, He knew events are in the Father's hands, and the kingdom of God is bigger than the gap between the ideal and the actual. All he could do was pray for his followers and those that would follow them—that's us and those we interact with. And not give up on them.

> Simon, Simon, Satan has asked to sift all of
> you as wheat. But I have prayed for you, Simon,
> that your faith may not fail. And when you have
> turned back, strengthen your brothers. (Luke
> 22:31–32 NIV)

How did the disciples handle the gap?

The disciples were expecting a political king; they all were thinking that the messiah would restore the nation and defeat the Romans. It was going to be glorious as this messiah or "Son of Man" was prophesied in Daniel that His kingdom will be absolute and never be destroyed.

> In my vision at night I looked, and there
> before me was one like a *son of man,* coming with
> the clouds of heaven. He approached the Ancient
> of Days and was led into his presence. He was
> given authority, glory and sovereign power; all
> nations and peoples of every language worshiped
> him. His dominion is an everlasting dominion
> that will not pass away, and his kingdom is one
> that will never be destroyed. (Daniel 7:13–14,
> NIV italics mine)

This is what they were looking for. Their expectations about this Son of Man and what He was to do were about to be crushed. This powerful Son of Man was beaten, mocked, dragged as a defeated king through the streets, and crucified as a common criminal. They reacted by denying, running, hiding, and were all stunned as the expectation of what they expected and the reality of what happened hit them. God was not done with these disciples nor was this a shock to Him. All would change three days after this Son of Man was crucified; things would change for these disciples and the world.

How can you handle the gap?

How you cope with that ever-present distance between your expectation of where people should be at and where they are at is crucial. The difference between the lines? Remember, it's God's box that is left on your porch, and what is inside is His, regardless of the person's position in that gap. Welcome to the human race and ministry. Guard your heart, and don't lose hope that God is not done with anyone. The Son of Man is still in charge, and things changed three days after the Son of Man was crucified.

Lesson from an Escalator in Tokyo

Airport empty stairs

Get ready, set, and follow the group.

Beware of the cult of the common. We have a tendency to conform to the group we are associated with. Many studies and experiments have been done to prove that people will usually conform to the group to be acceptable. To stand out from the group is usually not normal for most. Much easier to take your cues from the group to gain that identity and safety found in conforming. After all, it is easier to conform. If you gain your values and identity from the group, it's called *identity diffusion* or in a corporate structure *group think*. Based on two principles, (1) my reaction is by taking my cues from the group reaction and (2) not wanting to stand out. Never blindly follow the group for safety or security as the group can lead each other in the wrong directions. The group is not always a sign of the right way and is not always safe to follow.

> Enter through the narrow gate. For wide
> is the gate and broad is the road that leads to
> destruction, and many enter through it. But small
> is the gate and narrow the road that leads to life,
> and only a few find it. (Matthew 7:13–14 NIV)

A Lesson from an Escalator

I travel a lot to Asia, always stopping off in Tokyo, and this means changing to a new plane to finish the journey to Bangkok. Tokyo is always a busy airport, and you have to deplane and go through airport screening again. The problem is time. Usually, the time between flights is one to two hours. This brings about a need to be deplaned behind three hundred people all heading for the screening, which will develop a long line. To get to the screening area, you have to go up two floors via two escalators. The entire plane will take their place in line to go up the escalators. Next to them are stairs. I learned that I can go up the stairs and beat the whole group. This puts me in a good position to get ahead of the three hundred people for screening. It must be strange for the long lines of passengers, as they ride the escalators, to see one guy running past them up the stairs.

Why is no one taking the two sets of long stairs? Simply because that is the way the group is going, and people just have a strong tendency to take cues from each other. It's just easier to conform to the group, follow as all the others are, not stand out, and take the ride to the top of the stairs.

Good lesson for life. There are always those who can resist the group. These are called pioneers; we have all seen them. They have done things that we only look at from a distance, but they have impacted all of us in some way or another.

Always amazed at people who take the stairs. They always offer a different philosophy of ministry and life. The danger of the cult of the common is that we are funneled into the escalators of life, usually by following others and doing what has always been done before. In short, trapped in the cult of the common.

The Pharisees had their group, the Sadducees had their group, even the people had their group. Jesus stepped out of all the group identities of the day. As a result, He became a person who challenged all who hid in their group identity. He became a person who made decisions not on how it affected him, not on how it allowed him access and gain the approval of the groups of the day, but Jesus operated on principled decisions that made him stand apart from the groups. These principles were based on God's standards and purposes that he was called to fulfill. That didn't fit into the accepted methods of the day. That made him stand apart. Jesus developed a philosophy of ministry that was different.

I learned a lesson—there is a cost to the common in ministry.

Common ministry often leads to common results. Stand on biblical principles, and don't allow the group to always lead you. Pioneers were usually the minority and always stood out from the group.

Lesson from Guiding in Alaska

Above the bush cabin

Beware of defining today with yesterday.

I have a bush cabin in the remote Alaskan wilderness. I started guiding people from the lower forty-eight states and from all over the world into the wild backcountry of Alaska for an authentic Alaskan experience. It requires walking five miles through heavy brush and swamps. The trail is one that we hacked out with machetes. Over the years, I have guided people from all over the world. It is pure Alaskan wilderness with uncrossable glacial rivers, animals that aren't used to humans, grizzly bears that have no fear of anything, and the sudden shock of realizing you're not the top of the food chain anymore. You quickly realize that if you get lost, you're dead. It leaves one feeling pretty vulnerable. People who don't know me at all are totally dependent on me guiding them into the deep wilderness where I'm not top of the food chain either, but I do have a gun.

Orientation is important.

People have to orientate themselves in their present reality. The only way they can do that is by using the previous reality they are used to, using this as a way to make sense of the present place they are in that they are not used to. When in the wilds of Alaska, if their past ceases to be an adequate help to make sense of the new experience they are in, intellectually they can be in trouble. In their inability to have a safe framework in the present new reality, they will say things like, "These woods are just like what we have in Michigan" or "This reminds me of Rolla, Missouri," or "We have bears in Arkansas also" or "I hike a lot in Oklahoma, so no problem" or, like the girls from China, "How do you go to the bathroom out here?" Feeling disoriented, the person clings to the only thing they can orient themselves with, their past experiences. But those past experiences will not be sufficient to enable them to cope or adjust to the new reality. In fact, it can be a deterrent to the present. It's a slight form of culture shock because the person's previous culture or life is not sufficient to explain and adjust to the new one they are immersed in.

Just who am I? A crisis of identity.

Anytime you are in a new situation, you tend to make sense of it by the past. People don't like to live in a state of disequilibrium. It's really an identity crisis of "Who am I?" You find that a lot of our identity is gained from the environment that we are submerged in. Change that, and a crisis of "Who am I without all the support I have?" will surface. When you go overseas for a period, it can become a real struggle that is very disorienting. This is a major identity crisis. It's called culture shock. From one who experienced it, I can tell you it's real and no fun. I'm not sure how I got through it except through time. The way I reacted in midst of this struggle was to hide away or withdraw. To go outside was absolute chaos, and since I couldn't speak the language, it was pointless to make relationships, as the people didn't speak English. The honeymoon period in the first six months is when you don't mind looking like an idiot. The honeymoon period is over when you realize you are the village idiot, so it's better to stay inside and look out the window. You can always tell when someone is in culture shock. Their house is covered with items from their own country, pictures of places, and pictures of family a long way away are quickly brought out to show people that you really did have a life of importance before. Your thoughts are constantly about your home country, family, friends, food, water you can drink from the tap, a shower with hot water instead of a bucket, sports, electricity that was always there, aisles and aisles of food in stores, hardly ever worrying about deadly sicknesses, an electric stove instead of wood, the ease to get things like a driver's license, buses that weren't full of animals and people, dangerous roads, and other things you took for granted each day. In my home country, I never stood out. Here I always do. I was never the village idiot because there were always enough people around that someone else could fill that role. Then I read a verse that put it all in perspective.

Change is real.

> If they had been thinking of the country they had left, they would have had opportunity to return. Instead, they were longing for a better country—a heavenly one. Therefore God is not ashamed to be called their God, for he has prepared a city for them. (Hebrews 11:15–16 NIV)

I had to quit thinking of the past life or my past country. The past is only a step in building to the new. If you are in the new and constantly thinking of the past, you will find a reason to go back. This can be true in marriages, jobs, new relationships, new seasons in Christ, or any life situation. Change brings a crisis of identity.

In spiritual growth, our past can be a hindering factor for our future growth if we go back. It's a foundation to build on, not stay in.

The best way to cope in a new situation is to reconcile the fact that you are in a new place. Look to the new situation as new and realize you have a lot to learn, but you will learn and grow in new ways. When you learn about the new situation, you will feel comfortable again. In fact, you will expand your knowledge and experience, thus enriching you as a person. So let go of the structures of your past experiences and become a learner in the new, even if you look like the village idiot. Otherwise, you will find a reason to go back.

22

A Lesson from Logging

My Christian logging partner—1985

Do I exist for the church or does the church exist for me?

In our twenties, my wife and I moved to Greenwater, Washington, a small community in the Cascade Mountains north of Mount Rainier. I got a job logging, something that was totally new to me as I was raised in the suburbs north of Seattle. Logging towns are a culture unto themselves, made up of rugged guys who lived in a logging community and who often were part of generations of loggers. The clothing of a northwest logger is definable and unique.

Working in the woods meant I had to go to the logger's supply store and buy all new clothing. I was an outsider who had never worked a day in the woods.

At 5:00 a.m. my first morning, I showed up to meet the crew. It was dark and rainy. The others had been driving for thirty minutes, and I was their last stop. As I opened the door to the crew bus, the first thing that hit me were the smells from the crew. Those smells could have been used in WWI and ended the war early. Next thing I noticed was most were sleeping off hangovers. Others had bruises from the bar fights they had from the night before. I was a square peg in a round hole, no way to fake it. I took a seat and wished for the trees to fall on all of us and put an end to this. Maybe at least, a head-on accident with a logging truck that would put an end to this.

I had all the right clothes, but everything was brand new. I stood out like a flashing sign saying, "I'm the new greenhorn and haven't one dirt spot on my clothes yet."

I looked like a store front display for new logging clothes.

I have felt the same emotions when I was in a grocery store with a line of people behind me, and after a lengthy ringing up of items, the debit card is rejected. The silence and gasps of the people in line says it all. You're the center of attention, and you don't want it. Where is the rapture when you need it?

How I became a real logger.

What made me a real logger was the experience, not reading about it. There were no shortcuts. It was tough and rugged work. Often, I would wake up at night sweating, worrying about the next day's challenge. There were often near-death experiences, and many did get killed every year in the northwest logging. There was always a lot going on. You couldn't predict each day. In the next ten years, I learned all the techniques and methods of the technical and danger-ous high-lead logging in the Cascades. This knowledge came with a cost. The mistakes I made often brought bumps, bruises and several near-death escapes. Those gave me the ability to stand and learn to get through each day alive and log successfully. In short, I became an experienced logger.

When I got out of Bible school, I had to become aware that I was not trained for anything except basically teaching from a pulpit and setting people straight on doctrinal issues. In short, I was naïve to the reality of working with people who worked daily in the real world.

I looked like a store front display of a new Bible school graduate.

How you become effective for ministry.

It was through being immersed in people's lives that I became trained for the work of the ministry. In short, I was trained by the people I was leading. It's the people we serve that teach us the reality of ministry. The good, the bad, and the ugly situations make us fit for real ministry. We will never learn the realities of ministry until we have some bumps and bruises and near "death" escapes. Those are the very things that God can use to give me the ability to stand and stay in ministry. We have yet to learn how to survive through our own mistakes and come through them wiser. We need to get some wear and tear on our new clothes. There's a lot going on in churches you can't predict.

What will make us effective? The people we learn how to serve and minister. In fact, they make us effective by taking this brand-new person and giving us some chances to get bumps, bruises, and near-death experiences.

> While he lived on earth, anticipating death, Jesus cried out in pain and wept in sorrow as he offered up priestly prayers to God. Because he honored God, God answered him. Though he was God's Son, he learned trusting-obedience by what he suffered, just as we do. Then, having arrived at the full stature of his maturity and having been announced by God as high priest in the order of Melchizedek, he became the source of eternal salvation to all who believingly obey him. (Hebrews 5:7–10 MSG)

There are no shortcuts to effective ministry. Remember that the next time you feel betrayed, slandered, alone, and overworked. Now you're looking like an experienced veteran in ministry. It's the good, the better, and the best that will be developed in you.

Lesson from Sharing a Path

Share a unique experience.

We were missionaries in Nepal for almost four years in a remote village. We returned, and I enrolled in a master degree program at Wheaton College, near Chicago. It is south of Chicago and in suburbia. Through the area is what they call the prairie trail, a fifty-eight mile trail that has a branch in Wheaton. It is a restored thirty-foot-wide belt of nature that runs next to the busy city streets of Wheaton. It's a favorite for walkers, joggers, and bikers.

We used to walk and bike on this narrow piece of nature. I started noticing that while on this narrow gravel nature path. When passing someone on this path, both parties would make eye contact and say hi. Then I realized if we were twenty feet to the right walking on the city streets, you would not even look at each other. Why? What is the difference?

It's a matter of connection over a sharing of a unique experience. It is why military people are so tight. Why hobby clubs build such a bond. Why people will join clubs and have a shared identity over their focus. It is why if you're overseas and meet someone from your town or city, you have a special bond. I'm from Alaska, and if I am driving my car in the lower forty-eight states with Alaska license plates and parked in Walmart parking lots, I often find notes on my windshield saying, "Hi, we are from Alaska too."

I realized we connected over a *shared unique experience*. This became a revolutionary point for me in developing a philosophy of ministry. I sought to create unique experiences, not just preaching and teaching in a sterile classroom or from a pulpit, but create methods that would provide a unique experience that brings *connection*.

Development—the key to discipleship that lasts.

Thanks to my studies at Wheaton, I developed a philosophy of ministry that took me out of the usual church default methods of ministry or the usual idea of what ministry is. I was thirty years old when saved. I was a logger and got saved in a sinking fishing boat in a storm, off the coast in Alaska. It was never my way to take easy ways. I was a practical and hands-on guy that loved challenges and brought this into my ministry. I also noticed that most men were not changed or challenged by a sermon or a Sunday school hour. In short, the intellectual area did not reach most men who were loggers like I was or people who worked in lumber mills. My goal became to develop methods outside the common that would impact these types of people. Jesus, in His teaching with parables, often used the examples from nature to illustrate Christian truth. That became my model.

My goal became to develop the whole person, spiritually, physically, and challenge their character. My goal became to develop the whole individual. Next came my methods to do that. I didn't believe it would happen with just Bible studies, but character development takes a squeezing and being pressed through challenges. I started using the outdoors all summer. I would have a father-son or father-daughter eight-day canoe expedition, and at the end of sharing this unique experience, the bond and memories grew strong. I would do fifty-miler hikes for youth in the cascades, family canoe camping trips in nearby lakes, married eight-day canoe trips, nothing like a married couple paddling in a canoe together up a six-mile-long lake (remember sound carries, and you can hear all the arguing on which side to paddle on). I did short-term mission trips where the person stayed with a national host family. I did a father-son or father-daughter project where I had the fathers with their kids build a go-kart one winter to be raced in the spring when the snow melted.

I learned a lesson—create a unique ministry experience, and you will share a bond that is deep, personal, and always be remembered.

I still have connections with most of these people today. The youth who were thirteen to eighteen are now forty-year-olds with kids. I now do outdoor trips with some of them and their children, thirty years later. They never talked about some sermon I did twenty years ago but always about the trip we did where it rained seven days on a nine-day fifty-mile hike in the Cascades.

He spent three years living with, traveling with, and showing his followers; it was experiential not just lecturing. This created a shared unique experience among Him and His disciples.

You have the gift of teaching? Why only in classroom? You have the gift of serving? Why only inside church?

I learned a lesson—help families create a unique experience, and they will share a bond that is deep, personal, and always be remembered.

We share a unique experience with Jesus. We do not belong to the world as Jesus does not. We are on the same path.

> Just as I do not belong to the world, they do not belong to the world. Dedicate them to yourself by means of the truth; your word is truth. I sent them into the world, just as you sent me into the world. And for their sake I dedicate myself to you, in order that they, too, may be truly dedicated to you. "I pray not only for them, but also for those who believe in me because of their message. I pray that they may all be one. Father! May they be in us, just as you are in me and I am in you. May they be one, so that the world will believe that you sent me. I gave them the same glory you gave me, so that they may be one, just as you and I are one." (John 17:16–22 GNT)

A Lesson from a Band— You're Not a Real Star

A lesson—infiltrate don't dominate.

Man has an inner desire for power. Power brings control and prestige. In short, the top dog gets all the attention, and this can feed a sense of importance. I have experienced it in the secular realm. We all have. Sadly, I have seen it in the church. I have wondered why some people think the pastor title is a position of dominance and prestige to be set apart and above the ordinary person. Position of power and control, then history repeats itself. Power, authority, control, and then hurt and wounds, and people leave the church. Sorry to burst the bubbles, but I believe in the priesthood of the believer. I also think Jesus's style is the best. He lived with the common people, never dominated them. He led from the bottom up—not top down. It's not a title of power to lord over the church nor to select an office as the authority by which Jesus can build His church. The gifts are for building others up not for setting me up. We need church government, but the church is not a business corporation which has a top-down flowchart that make the higher position on the flowchart of more importance. Everyone is equal at the foot of the cross. Different gifts and talents, but they are given to serve not dominate.

Infiltration versus Domination

Jesus's style was different. He infiltrated the human race; he didn't dominate. Sure, His followers were climbing over themselves to get dominance over others. They wanted to gain position, power, authority, and control over others to be served not serve. These guys hadn't yet understood the real Jesus and had no clue about the nature of His kingdom. Even the mom of two sons tried to get her sons into big positions.

It was about that time that the mother of the Zebedee brothers came with her two sons and knelt before Jesus with a request.

"What do you want?" Jesus asked.

She said, "Give your word that these two sons of mine will be awarded the highest places of honor in your kingdom, one at your right hand, one at your left hand." Jesus responded, "You have no idea what you're asking." And he said to James and John, "Are you capable of drinking the cup that I'm about to drink?"

They said, "Sure, why not?"

Jesus said, "Come to think of it, you *are* going to drink my cup. But as to awarding places of honor, that's not my business. My Father is taking care of that."

When the ten others heard about this, they lost their tempers, thoroughly disgusted with the two brothers. So Jesus got them together to set-tle things down. He said, "You've observed how godless rulers throw their weight around, how quickly a little power goes to their heads. It's not going to be that way with you. Whoever wants to be great must become a servant." Whoever wants to be first among you must be your slave. That is what the Son of Man has done: He came to

serve, not be served—and then to give away his
life in exchange for the many who are held hos-
tage. (Matthew 20:20–28 MSG)

The ease that one finds in going from a life of the ordinary and
often mundane into a pulpit, finding attention and adoration from
so many, can be very addicting to human nature. Every Sunday, the
focus is on the pulpit and, hence, the special person filling it; the
person can forget they had an exciting life of selling life insurance or
digging holes with a backhoe before ministry. In my case, it was logging. After another tremendous sermon and the usual rush of people
to affirm that it was the best sermon yet, we can soon forget what our
position is really about.

We can develop the star syndrome.

For two hours each Sunday, I'm at the center of attention, adoration, all lights on me; it's my mic, it's my pulpit, it's "my house,"
it's my worship team to get people ready for the word. This can be
very addicting and dangerous. Even the mission field can be a dangerous place to feed our view of self, as being from the West auto-
matically puts you in a higher position above the average person in
that country.

We would do well to follow the example of Marcus Aurelius.
While ruling Rome, Marcus Aurelius was concerned he might let his
power go to his head. As legend has it, Aurelius hired a servant to lit-
erally follow him around as he walked the empire's streets. Every time
a citizen bowed a knee or called out a word of praise, Marcus Aurelius
instructed the servant to whisper this reminder in his ear, "You're just
a man. You're just a man."

Our goal is not for fame nor control or power over others. Our
position in the church means a higher call to serve not be served. Our
effectiveness cannot be measured in our popularity but rather how
we serve people in Christ. Don't let this period of attention become
addicting and go to your head. Infiltrate don't dominate. Lead from
the bottom up not top down.

We, like Marcus, should have a person to stand at the altar
and after each incredible sermon we preach on Sunday whisper a

reminder in our ear, "You're just a servant not a star, and remember, you're just one step away from disappearing back into an office to sell life insurance or log again." Even your mom won't be able get you out of it.

Lesson from a Snow Cave

Sometimes you have to dig to survive.

Climbing can bring all kinds of unknowns, all kinds of unexpected situations. Most of the time you are not in control of events; events control you. Survival depends on your actions, determination, character, and skill. It also depends on your team. A rope team is only as fast as the weakest member. I found this out climbing Mount Hood in Oregon on a winter ascent. *Mount Hood* is the highest peak (11,239 feet) in Oregon, and the fourth highest peak in the Cascade Range. A lot of things can change on this mountain in the winter.

There were five of us, and we wanted to climb Mount Hood in January. We lived in Seattle, and this is near Portland, Oregon. We had a nice break in the weather, clear and cold, so we grabbed our winter gear, snowshoes, and excitement and drove south. As we arrived at the parking lot on the mountain, it was clear, cold, and windy. We started our ascent on snowshoes and climbed to the nine thousand foot level where we didn't need snowshoes anymore, so we left them where we could pick them up on the way down. Climbing on, we worked our way up to the upper mountain.

The wind picked up, and all of a sudden, we were hit with a winter storm of incredible force. The problem was we were exposed on the upper mountain below the summit with no protection from the wind or weather. Temperatures dropped to below 20, and the snow was horizontally hitting us in the face with a sixty miles per hour wind. You could not hear someone unless you yelled in their face. We couldn't descend as that would have been almost impossible and certain death. We only had one thing to do; try to prolong our death by surviving as best we could. Since it was a day climb, we had no tents (in this wind, we couldn't have used one anyway) and only one sleeping bag for an emergency need. We always had a shovel in the winter in case of needing an emergency shelter dug in the snow. We all had an ice axe.

Two climbers on the team were starting to get extremely cold. We put them into the one sleeping bag, and they sat exposed on the mountain in a sixty miles per hour wind at -20. They were getting colder. There was no way we could go down now. We would have gotten lost on the vast expanse of this mountain slope, and the two climbers were too weak. It was a total whiteout, so think you could not see twenty feet. We only had one chance. We had to dig a snow cave to survive. So we started digging into the side of the mountain. It takes a big cave for five guys, but we started. With two of our team dropped out and could not function well, it left three of us to dig. We were digging for our very survival. We had no idea how long the storm would last, but we had to get out of the wind on this exposed icy and snowy mountain. We finally got it big enough for five of us. In we went for the longest, sleepless, coldest, and most miserable night of our lives. Inside temperature was above freezing and with a candle or stove would get up around 38. Finally, it got light enough to look outside the cave. The wind had died down enough so we could walk, and we decided to head down. After sitting in an ice cave all night, all the moisture condensed on us, so our clothes and jackets were wet. Immediately exiting the ice cave, we found our wet clothes freeze and become stiff. We started down, but as it was still whiteout conditions, we had to stay together because you could not see more than twenty feet, and if someone got lost up here, you could never find them or hear them as the wind was still blowing hard. A person would just wander off alone into the blizzard until they collapsed. The other issue was which direction to head down. This part of the mountain is notoriously famous for people getting lost coming down as it is a vast expanse with no markers. You have to come out at Timberline Lodge where the road and cars are. Off a few degrees, and you end up lost in the tree line. We never found the snowshoes we had left, but the wind made the snow hard and easy to walk on. Off we went in the best heading we could guess. We looked like five overworked slaves marching off to the Roman salt mines, not sure if we will survive another day.

Since this was before GPS, we only could go by a compass heading. After four hours of walking, we hit the tree line but no road! Since the lodge is above tree line, we knew we missed it. We didn't know if it was to our left or right. We walked a little farther and heard the best sound ever—a car! This meant the road. We got to the road absolutely exhausted and walked back up the road a mile to the parking lot to our car. We missed it by one mile, but fortunately, we meandered off the south side of the lodge area, which is where the road comes up to the lodge. If we had missed it on the north side, well let's just say my two sons probably would not be here today either.

Sometimes in the Christian life, all you can do is dig for survival. Paul experienced it, others have also through being tortured and killed. All of us will get caught in a storm, persecution, betrayal, family problems, marital storms, death of a loved one, sickness, but remember, Jesus is a shelter. Regardless of what is going on around us, He is the only shelter for safety.

> I would hurry to my place of shelter, far
> from the tempest and storm. (Psalm 55:8 NIV)

> Whoever dwells in the shelter of the Most
> High will rest in the shadow of the Almighty.
> (Psalm 91)

Sometimes in a storm of life, you have to dig to find a shelter—Jesus is our shelter. Dig as though your life depended on it. Sometimes you're not just digging for yourself but for others also.

A Lesson on a Canoe Expedition and Turning Hearts

Process versus goal.

While at Wheaton graduate school, I found a verse that changed my ministry philosophy and focus. It was in Malachi.

> See, I will send the prophet Elijah to you before that great and dreadful day of the Lord comes. He will turn the hearts of the parents to their children, and the hearts of the children to their parents; or else I will come and strike the land with total destruction. (Malachi 4:5–6 NIV)

I wanted to work with fathers and sons or daughters in turning their hearts to each other. I realized you could use the outdoors to accomplish this. I heard about an eight-day wilderness canoe trip that was rated one of the top ten canoe trips in the world called Bowron Lakes Provincial Park. It was located in western Canada above Washington State and would only take us twelve hours of driving. It was a challenging trip, so I got seven dads and seven young sons to do the first trip. It would be seven canoes and fourteen people. Since I was a canoeist and loved to camp, it seemed like a great method to "turn the fathers' hearts to children and children's hearts to fathers." Bowron Lakes is an interconnected one-hundred-mile chain of lakes forming a square with rivers connecting the lakes and several one-mile trail portages. You start and end at the same lake. Putting a father and son or daughter together in a canoe for eight days is a great way to build relationships, memories, and partnering together. They paddle as a team on this expedition canoe trip into the wilderness of Canada.

What is more important, the process or the goal?

The advantage of using a wilderness canoe trip to build relationship with the father and son or daughter was that neither knew what to do. I had a wide range of dads, dentists, bankers, accountants, policemen, all kinds of professionals on these trips. They controlled their world, they knew what to do in their businesses, but out here, they became a learner and equal with their youth. They were not skilled in canoeing. They had never done an eight-day wilderness canoe trip before. Both were vulnerable, and both were learners on the same team. In short, this was perfect for building memories and bringing walls down. They had to work together as a team; they depended on each other for the first time in a unique experience.

On one trip as we got close to the park, a local radio station was reporting that a couple had been airlifted off the Bowron Lakes because they were attacked by a grizzly bear. The guy was in critical condition, and the girl was mauled but not as seriously. This was where we were headed for the next eight days. They got nervous, and you could tell dads were nervous because they started joking about bears or the potential of an attack. The kids were cooler about it because they had no concept of what a bear can do to a twelve-year-old. We pulled into the park headquarters and set up our first night's camp there in the campground before starting the canoe circuit in the morning. As we pulled in, there were two big yellow barrels with trap gates on the front. They were bear traps. There were also signs saying they are trying to catch two bears in the area, so don't sleep with your food. I calmly told them they were the food. Their eyes said it all. "What have I gotten myself and son into?" I reassured them as best I could that out of fourteen of us, it would be reasonable to assume thirteen would get home. The percentage for survival was pretty high. Actually, this was the wilderness, and you can't control it. You must survive by skill and the group helping each other. It was perfect for turning hearts to each other. That night, they all slept in the van except my son and I and another brave father and son. The next day, off into the wilderness we went. We began our canoeing on the circuit with no more van for protection. There were just little nylon tents with two tasty treats inside. Most would be lying awake hearing every sound in the night.

This is where I realized the process is most important and the goal is secondary. If the goal was to finish the canoe circuit, you could paddle hard and complete it, but you would miss things on the way. During the process, growth happens. Fears are conquered, courage developed, confidence built, memories made, and new skills are learned. Each day paddling along the lake together, they would be seeing the mountains, seeing the animals, catching fish, discussing things, and both would be responsible for the day's achievements. One goal was to complete the one-hundred-mile canoe circuit, but using this goal to develop relationships during process was the ultimate goal. Even if we couldn't finish the canoe circuit, the process still happened. Each night around the campfire, we would give Christian testimonies, talk, and have Bible studies. Each day they worked together as a team as they launched out into the new adventures each day held. At the end of the trip, it was always amazing to see that the relationships had become stronger between the father and son or daughter.

One of the dads wasn't the best canoeist, being a novice at canoeing, and the long daily six-hour days would take a toll on him. This provided me with perfect video-filming opportunities. When he reached the shore each night, he would crawl onto the beach and collapse lying on his back moaning. This was my moment to film him. He would be snoring in his tent, and I usually caught that in the movie I was making. I loved to capture on video what they wished I wouldn't. I would also film the skinny twelve-year-old youths. After the trip, I would make copies and give them to each dad for memories of a great trip.

Several years ago I was visiting in the area where we lived at that time and where we had our ministry. I happened to see this guy's wife. I asked how he was, and she said he had just recently died from cancer. The son he had taken was twelve at that time of the trip but now was thirty with a son himself. She said, "You know what we did? We had the funeral service, then afterward just the family came back to the house, and we watched the Bowron Lakes trip video."

We did finish the goal and got to the end eight days later, but what happened in those eight days will never be forgotten. The process allowed for the building of family memories on that trip, and they have it on film for all the generations. If you want to join the generations, make memories, and be process-oriented. Goals will happen.

27

Lesson about Cow Dung, Babies, and Change

Nepali women on the trail

Live in a way to cause envy.

Cow dung is generally not a favorite topic of conversation. Cow dung is worth discussing though. In Nepal, it's a useful material and helps Nepalese in a variety of ways. It's also a plentiful and renewable resource because most villagers have cows or water buffaloes. It's very valuable when used correctly. It's a shame when it's wasted. It's dangerous when used wrongly.

Cow dung has a lot of daily benefits for all of us. Actually, this probably isn't true for anyone in the West, but it is true for the village where we lived in the remote mountains of Nepal. Cow dung was dried and used to cook as firewood was scarce. It was used as fertilizer for their crops. They would mix it with water and mud to smooth the mud floor each day and mud walls of the small village houses. Sadly, using cow dung was not a skill my wife possessed but soon learned in the village. You would never find this at Lowe's as a floor finisher.

However, there was one use that often brought death to newborn babies.

We lived in a small village that thirty-five years ago didn't even have matches or lights. The ladies did not have mirrors. It was like walking back in time two thousand years. The ladies would often come down to our house and ask my wife to bring a mirror so they could look at themselves.

Childbirth was and is incredibly hard for women in these remote villages and very dangerous. The nearest hospital was a five-day walk, and if they had complications for several days, they would have to be carried the entire way to the hospital five days away. Often, we would see them being carried for days to the hospital for complications during a birth that could not be dealt with by village women who helped during birth. Absolutely, one of the most horrifying sights you could see and hear on the trail.

If they delivered a baby in this village, they had a tradition that they thought was required for the sake of the newborn. Who knows when it started or how long they had been doing it. No one questioned it. They just accepted it as a necessary ritual for the health of the newborn.

Everyone wants a healthy baby. Their fear was evil spirits and the vulnerability of the newborn. They believed that evil spirits would enter any holes in the body. To keep evil spirits out, they would put fresh cow dung on the umbilical cord when they cut it at birth. Because the cow is worshipped as holy in Nepal, their thinking was it would prevent evil spirits from doing harm to the baby. Spirits could not enter if the newly cut umbilical cord was sealed with the holy cow dung. The result for the infant was often death from tetanus. In our village, it was a usual occurrence to hear the wailing of a mother over the death of the baby. Infant death was common, and 40% of the children born would die before the age of five. Many times through traditions that became passed on. Hundreds of years ago rubbing cow dung became an entrenched tradition that is still practiced regardless of what the villagers were told or taught by the missionary nurses that our project would bring up to train village midwives. The inherited method that they thought would bring life—became a tradition that brought death.

I learned a big lesson. Change is hard for people, even if the old way means death.

A huge question we wrestled with in community development work was "What will cause people to change?"

We wrestle with that in churches also. We preach and teach how to live a better life, and yet people often remain in their old way. This can be true of those doing the preaching and teaching. So no one can point fingers. One thing for sure, change is hard. Even if the old way isn't working.

I started drinking alcohol in high school, and by thirty, I was an alcoholic. Before I became a Christian, I knew I was addicted and could not quit. I had tried several times to quit to no avail. What caused me to wake up to the idea of this needed change in my life to quit drinking? It was my first close encounter with a Christian man who lived in our neighborhood. We would have them over to our house, and I noticed he never drank alcohol and he still had a good time. Ah, sweet envy, it can begin a process of wanting change.

I saw the potential and was envious of the freedom he had. I wanted change. Then God by His power intervened when I was a new Christian. One Saturday morning, I felt I should not drink. I prayed, "God if you want me to quit, you have to take it away, and I promise I will never touch it again, and use it in our families as a witness." I got up off my knees delivered from alcohol completely. I had no withdrawals and have never touched nor wanted it for thirty-six years. It was the first time I ever felt God's power. He did use this testimony in our families.

Change happens often when we are in a crisis. God will often use others to spark envy and start a process of change. In other words, someone is a light on the hill. It really begins through relationships with others. I was offered hope and wanted that. In short, I became envious of my neighbor's freedom in Christ, and God changed me by his power. My neighbor was salt and did not even know it. Envious of a couple with a solid marriage? Envious of people with an ability to trust God? Envious of those who walk in forgiveness? On and on it can go. We are presented with the truths of the Bible through lives we run into that reveal it.

Paul had the same idea in Romans 11:13–14, "I am talking to you Gentiles. Inasmuch as I am the apostle to the Gentiles, I take pride in my ministry in the hope that I may somehow arouse my own people to envy and save some of them."

Want change in people? Be *relationalistic* not *rationalistic*. Let your life reveal Christ in your relationships.

Lesson from the Kathmandu Deluxe Express Bus

Be careful of the first people that approach you.

I was assured this was the best, most comfortable, and the fastest bus to Kathmandu from Pokhara. It was our first time traveling by bus in Nepal, and the bus park was a confusing situation. There were thousands of people everywhere, hundreds of buses, and destinations in Nepali being screamed from every direction. We might as well have been on another planet. We were quickly approached by a fast-talking Nepali in broken English asking us where we are going. I said Kathmandu. He said the best bus was the Kathmandu Deluxe Express. This sounded perfect. A fast, comfortable deluxe bus to Kathmandu, at least, according to this guy it was. We bought two tickets on the Kathmandu Deluxe Express.

It was our first time in Pokhara, which was a long eight-hour bus ride from Kathmandu. We visited Pokhara to meet with the mission we were going to join after finishing Bible school the following year. Now we were headed back to Kathmandu. I learned a hard lesson that day, and unfortunately, my wife did also. You can't judge a bus by the name, and be careful about the first person that approaches you to sell something, especially in a confusing situation.

At that time, travel between Kathmandu and Pokhara was long and dusty. A quick trip took eight hours or a whole day. You would be covered in dust because no buses had AC, and the windows would be open. You would want to make that trip as easy, comfortable, and as fast as possible. We had heard of a tourist bus called Swiss Travels, which only hauled tourists. The Kathmandu Deluxe Express did the exact opposite. It was the local bus. There is a difference. Not realizing the difference, I bought tickets on the Kathmandu Deluxe Express, and soon this old falling-apart bus pulled up. Nepalis started fighting to get on. Not just Nepalis themselves, but they were carrying chickens, a few goats, and other items. I asked the Nepali outside collecting tickets which bus was the Kathmandu Deluxe Express bus. He said, "This one." I knew then I'd made the biggest mistake of our short lives. We got on, or forced our way on, to our seats, which were wood benches with a covering of cloth that had holes in it with stains from who knows what. I could see the ground through the rusted-out parts of the floor. I didn't even want to think of the conditions of the brakes or tires. I knew that buses regularly went off the steep cliffs and tumbled down the banks into the river below. Not many ever survived. So we sat down while people kept getting on. The aisle soon was packed full of sweating people standing looking down at us. To my right was a Nepali with a young goat that was looking at me, to my left was my wife who was also looking at me. Neither stare was of comfort. One was of a frightened animal going to be sacrificed and eaten, the other was from a wife who was about to embark on this miserable day's journey. I was wishing that the hole in the floor was big enough for me to escape through.

To make matters worse, as we were sitting there waiting for any kind of movement, the brand-new Swiss Travel Bus pulled up next to us. There were cushioned seats that reclined and a headrest with a nice white covering. Each person had their own seat, no people were standing, and there were no animals. They were all tourists with smiles, unlike in our bus. They looked over at us and saw two westerners in the midst of a crowd of Nepalis and animals. You could see by their looks that their pity for us was real. Our jealousy for them was also real. Off they went nonstop for their seven-hour trip to Kathmandu while we stopped in every town and village along the way to let people off and pick up more passengers. It was a twelve-hour ride we never forgot. So much for the Kathmandu Deluxe Express.

It was a lesson in not jumping at the first person that approaches you especially in a confusing situation. Before moving to a remote village in the Himalaya Mountains of Nepal, an older missionary gave us some advice which I always remembered. Don't jump at the first person that comes to you for attention as the real leaders of the village are more reserved. Those that want the attention are usually the first to approach you. The real leaders are going to be more cautious and reserved, and they are the ones with the most influence.

I have found the same goes for ministry in church work. When coming to a new church, we found that the ones who first approached often had an axe to grind with the previous church leaders or an agenda that was ignored, and they wanted to sell it to the new people.

> The first speech in a court case is always convincing—until the cross-examination starts! (Proverbs 18:17 MSG)

When I take groups to the mission field for a short mission trip, I stress the need to be careful about committing to projects or making promises to people that ask for things. Many times, the people from the west are viewed as a money source, and you find yourself overflowing with people coming up to you. It's better not to promise things to people than to promise and not fulfill the promise.

> Do not be one who shakes hands in pledge or puts up security for debts; if you lack the means to pay, your very bed will be snatched from under you. (Proverbs 22:26–27 NIV)

Any new church we go to or any trip to another country can become that confusing situation where we can make wrong choices or make wrong promises.

As you step into a new situation, you need to be careful and not make any major decisions until you have been there a good amount of time. It takes time to gain trust and see what has been going on before you understand what is going on today. If you're not careful, you will find yourself a target for someone's opportunity and find yourself on the Kathmandu Deluxe Express, full of misery and problems down the road.

Lesson on Giving Up

*I*t's easy to die for something, harder to give it up.

Throughout history we find people willingly to die for land, houses, political movements, possessions, and their countries. We see examples of communists willing to die for their beliefs and soldiers willing to die for those that lead them. What mother would not lay down her life for her kids if they were attacked or a husband for his family?

Seems like history proves people will die for something they hold dear. Let me rephrase this question in a different context.

Would you be willing to give up the very person you were willing to die for? Willing to give up into God's hands what you hold dearest? To perhaps lose the very thing you were willing to die for?

It is hard to give up.

Yet that is the very thing that brings freedom. In fact, Jesus says if you give up family, friends, land for my sake, receive a hundred times more. It's crucial not only to trust but to entrust all to Him.

> And Jesus replied, "Let me assure you that no one has ever given up anything—home, brothers, sisters, mother, father, children, or property—for love of me and to tell others the Good News, who won't be given back, a hundred times over, homes, brothers, sisters, mothers, children, and land—with persecutions!" (Mark 10:29–31 TLB)

> In the same way, those of you who do not
> give up everything you have cannot be my disci-
> ples. (Luke 14:33 NIV)

After finishing Bible college in Canada, we were accepted into a mission that was based out of Philadelphia, Pennsylvania. They would send us to the country of Nepal as missionaries to serve with another long-established mission already working in Nepal. While in Philadelphia, we were told that a doctor and his family had just returned from the same mission in Nepal that we would be working with. We spent a day driving down to Richmond, Virginia for a visit with them. It would be good to get firsthand information from them about working in Nepal.

When we arrived at their house, we learned what giving up really meant.

Upon entering the house, there was the doctor, his wife, and their eight-year-old daughter. They had just been in Nepal two months and suddenly returned home. In the house, I saw a picture of a four-year-old boy and asked who this was as he wasn't around. They said he was their son who just died in Nepal. They said he woke with a headache and was dead by that night. They came home shattered and broken. I looked at my two-year-old and my eight-year-old son and thought, *I'm going to lose them!* This family just had lost their son. He was a doctor and couldn't save his son. I'm an ex-logger. He was in Pokhara where there is one of the best hospitals in western Nepal. We were going to be in a remote village that would take three or four days of trekking to reach. I had a choice to make. Was I willing to give up my sons and stay safe in America or still go to Nepal uncertain of any outcome?

I learned how hard it was to really give up.

I looked at my sons and had a decision to make—a decision of trust. Was I willing to give up my sons to go to Nepal? Was I willing to live in trust that no matter what happens. Did I believe that He is a good God and has a plan? If I *trust*, then I have to *entrust* all I have and do to Him. He just wants us to live by faith.

The famous faith chapter in (Hebrews 11:32–35 NIV):

> And what more shall I say? I do not have time to tell about Gideon, Barak, Samson and Jephthah, about David and Samuel and the prophets, who through faith conquered kingdoms, administered justice, and gained what was promised; who shut the mouths of lions, quenched the fury of the flames, and escaped the edge of the sword; whose weakness was turned to strength; and who became powerful in battle and routed foreign armies. Women received back their dead, raised to life again.

Sounds awesome, this faith. Dead raised, routed armies, conquered kingdoms. Then it goes on to give examples of other's faith and giving up.

> There were others who were tortured, refusing to be released so that they might gain an even better resurrection. Some faced jeers and flogging, and even chains and imprisonment. They were put to death by stoning; they were sawed in two; they were killed by the sword. They went about in sheepskins and goatskins, destitute, persecuted and mistreated—the world was not worthy of them. They wandered in deserts and mountains, living in caves and in holes in the ground. These were all commended for their faith, yet none of them received what had been promised, since God had planned something better for us so that only together with us would they be made perfect. (Hebrews 11:35b–40 NIV)

By faith, some tortured, stoned, sawed in two.

I had a decision to make. Not a decision of an adrenaline-filled moment to defend against an attack. It was premeditated, thoughtful, starting to count the cost moment that required more than just trust. Would I entrust? I decided then that I would give all to him, even my sons. There were no guarantees of safe returns as I was looking at a family that had given up all to go to Nepal, and their son had died.

This was a major turning point. We went to Nepal, and we all survived.

We went to Nepal by faith and didn't lose a son. They went to Nepal by faith and lost a son. Who can explain it? No one. We are just called to trust and then to entrust to him all I that I have.

Sometimes, you have to be all-in to unlock your destiny. You can trust, but can you entrust? It's an amazing principle that as we give up, we receive more, a lot more!

My first of many lessons on what giving up really means.

A Lesson from a Canoe Rescue

Rescue a drowning person from the boat.

I was an avid white water canoeist when I was young. I loved to canoe the many rivers in Washington State. Once I was with a group of others canoeing a river in northern Washington State. We were doing great until we hit a rough section with large rapids. I went through a rough section first and was able to navigate the river successfully. I pulled over to watch the others navigate this section. While watching from shore, another canoe flipped over and the two people were suddenly trying to swim in a big turbulent river. One of the guys in the canoe did not want a life jacket and was not wearing one. I could see he was quickly in trouble as he could not fight the strong turbulent cold water. I watched as his head disappeared under the water twice. Just as he was floating by in the middle of the river, I saw he was helpless and out of strength. I quickly got in a canoe and paddled out to get him. As I approached, his head went under again. He came up and barely had enough strength to swim. I yelled for him to grab the canoe, and I would paddle him to the shore. He did and his life was spared.

The point is it would not have done any good if I had been in the river struggling too. We both would have drowned. Rescue was only possible because I was in a position of strength and safety while he was in the river.

We can minister from our weak areas only when we have gained victory over them. If we try to minister while we are in them, we will not help ourselves or others.

Be careful to minister *from* your weakness and not *in* them.

There is a tendency to minister in our weak areas or hurts. It's fresh and a focus we are currently in. We are struggling and realize the problem so we can transfer victory in that area by preaching or hiding it through ministry of truth to others. "I know what I should do and what you should too."

Be careful about my gifts always being used in my hurts and not from them.

If we were abused and never experienced love, our main focus can be an emphasis on God's love. While true, it becomes unbalanced and not the full council of God's character. If we came from a past life of sinful excesses, we can lean toward legalism and control as a way to prevent others from doing what I did. It is a recipe for disaster in raising kids this way and cloaking it in religion.

If I have deep unresolved insecurities, I can always question people's motives and tend toward "one-man shows."

As a new Christian, I remember a well-known TV preacher always preaching against sexual sin only to find out he was deeply engaged in sexual sin and had to step down. It was a weak area he was struggling with. Preaching against it to others through guilt was a way to self-atone for it by his avid, raging against the very thing he was doing. He could easily judge it in others and always had an emphasis on God's mercy.

Other leaders still preaching while in the midst of sexual sin themselves are constantly preaching about God's love and forgiveness, tempering their message with their need for grace on to everyone else.

Our weak areas become our strengths when we get victory. Healing can put them in proper perspective. Then we can minister *from* them and not *in* them. Without victory, they become dangerous for us to minister in. It is "do as I say, not do as I do." We can minister from our weak areas only when we have gained victory and healing over them. If we try to minister while in them, we will not help ourselves or others.

God's grace is the power for salvation but also the power to live victorious. It teaches us to say *no* to sin.

> For the grace of God has appeared that offers salvation to all people. It teaches us to say "No" to ungodliness and worldly passions, and to live self-controlled, upright and godly lives in this present age, while we wait for the blessed hope— the appearing of the glory of our great God and Savior, Jesus Christ. (Titus 2:11–13 NIV)

His grace is available to empower us to minister *from* our weak areas. We are not abandoned to minister *in* them. That's when our weak areas become strong when we can say, "I was there also, I was stuck in sin," but by God's grace I was set free and you can be also. People need to see examples of overcoming by His grace—that is hope.

Drowning people need someone in the canoe helping them out of the river not drowning in the river with them. Live in a way that reveals the power of God's grace and in a position that can pull people up and out of darkness.

Healed people can offer healing.

Lesson from Staying Overnight at Suzy's House

Or surviving the Peter principle.

"I really, really, really want to stay overnight at Suzy's house. Please! Let me stay!" It's your ten-year-old daughter pleading with you to stay at her friend's house overnight.

You answer, "But you've never stayed away from home before."

Your daughter replies, "I know, but the biggest thing in the world I want now is to stay overnight at Suzy's." So you allow her to stay at Suzy's house.

How things change.

About 11:00 p.m., you get a call from Suzy's parents. They put your daughter on the phone, and she says, "I want to come home."

You look at the clock and say, "I thought the biggest thing in the world you wanted was to stay at Suzy's house?"

She answers, "Yes, but now the biggest thing in the world I want is to come home."

Most of us will go through what I call the Peter principle.

> "Simon, Simon, Satan has asked to sift all of you as wheat. But I have prayed for you, Simon, that your faith may not fail. And when you have turned back, strengthen your brothers."

But he replied, "Lord, I am ready to go with you to prison and to death."

Jesus answered, "I tell you, Peter, before the rooster crows today, you will deny three times that you know me." (Luke 22:31–34 NIV)

This is Peter boasting he would not betray Jesus. He adamantly says he will stand with Him to prison and death. He was soon going to face his own weakness. He was destined for a setback, but that was going to be used as a setup for Peter.

When I was in Bible school getting ready to go to Nepal as a missionary, I would often say how I was ready to die for the Nepali people. I knew we were called to Nepal. While sitting around the comfortable school cafeteria complaining about the coffee, it was easy to tell other students about my willingness to die for the Nepali people. In fact, I even said I would give up my USA citizenship if it meant fulfilling my call. The biggest thing in the world I wanted was to go live in Nepal. I was emotionally committed and driven but hadn't been living there yet. The beginning of any call of God is an important stage because emotions will give us the energy and drive to get us to a place or calling, but emotions will not be sufficient to keep us at Suzy's house.

Then we moved to Nepal. About five to twelve months in the village, I came to grips with the Peter principle. Willing to die for the Nepali villagers? I didn't even like them anymore. The Nepali kids were always stealing from my kids. I wanted to get a big dog in the yard to keep them out. Some of the Nepali village men would take financial advantage of me. I didn't know the language. I couldn't talk to them. I got tired of looking like the village idiot smiling when they talked to me and looking like I understood. I knew they knew I didn't understand because their head would shake as they walked away. The food no longer had a novelty to it. I was sick of rice for breakfast, rice for lunch, rice for dinner. If you wanted a snack before bed, just pull out some rice. In the midst of culture shock, I found myself facing the reality of myself. Die for them? Ha! I didn't even want to live among them. I wanted to go home, and I was dreaming of ways to get kicked out of the country. After all, an honorable way to go home is to be kicked out for sharing the gospel. Maybe to speed up getting kicked out, I could stand in front of the village police station with a sign board saying, "Repent! The end is near." It was for me.

The biggest thing that I wanted in Bible school was going to Nepal. Now, in the midst of culture shock, homesickness, lack of food, no contact with family, cooking on a fire, washing clothes in the river, and just plain tired of being sick all the time, the biggest thing I wanted to do was go home. I had no thoughts about changing citizenship. In fact, I was hanging on to my passport like a person on the sinking *Titanic* with the last life jacket. Now to just get back home in one piece, in three years.

Ah! The Peter principle!

Like Peter, it was a huge blow to self but a necessary one. The emotions aren't enough to keep anyone in their calling. Like Peter, I needed to come to the end of myself and fleshly boasting. Like Peter, I needed to reveal Christ's power not mine. After twelve months, I finally turned the corner and began operating in Christ's strength not mine. No more boasting, and no more bragging. Now it was just plain trying to help these people. I was humbled.

Peter did return but not in his own strength. He was brought low, and this allowed him to be used from on high. He had the wrong idea about almost everything. This needed to be changed, and the only way to change was to see the folly of his own abilities. The kingdom principles could not be built on Peter's principles but could only be built on Christ's principles.

I did return but not in my own strength. I was brought low to be used from on high.

Next time you find yourself in the Peter principle, remember it's necessary and just the beginning of your being used by Jesus. It could be your marriage, the new church, the old church, your job, the in-laws, or your kids.

It's never the end when we come to the end of me. It's just the beginning. Remember, *a setback in Him is a setup for Him.*

32

Lesson from Making a Trail

The "trail" into the bush cabin

In the ministry of being a follower, we all follow someone who can lead others.

To get to my Alaska bush cabin, you have to walk through six miles of a hand-made trail that took us three days to hack out of the thick, tall alder brush. The trail is narrow and requires some balance and grace. The thing about the Alaska alder is the density and how tall they get. They are one to four inches in diameter, and they grow ten feet tall. You can't see more than twenty feet around you, and they grow over your head so that the sky is blocked. In this country, if you get lost in the wilderness in Alaska and you are in the alders, you're either dead or soon will be. It's what makes Alaska so unique and foreboding. I have often picked up young hitchhikers from the lower states or Europe who dreamed of coming to Alaska in the summer, getting off the road, and disappearing into the solitude of Alaska's nature. The problem is the alders and rivers. They soon discover you just can't stop on the side of the road and take off into the hills as you can in the lower forty-eight states. They soon become road-bound or look for an established area that offers hiking trails.

That's what makes my cabin in the Alaska wilderness so unique. Most wilderness cabins you have to fly into. I guide people out to my cabin on our hand-made six-mile trail. It took us over three days to hack a trail through the alders. If you were on the highway to Fairbanks and looked over towards Denali National Park, you would never believe that six miles west at the foot of the mountains is a cabin that you can walk to. The only reason it's accessible is because there is a trail that was hacked out with machetes and I know how to find it and stay on it. It can be very rough for some as it has muddy areas, swampy areas, and the alder patches you have to go through. It is not a smooth trail like a park trail. It's full of obstacles, and you have to watch where you walk.

On one trip, I had a group from Missouri. One guy in particular started complaining about the trail because it wasn't like the one he had in a park down in Missouri. So unknowing to him, I took him off the trail into the alders in a curve that fifteen minutes later had us back on the trail. He never complained again as he realized the advantage of the rough hand-made trail compared to fighting the alders without one.

You realize the trail that we put in makes an easier way in the wilderness for those who follow. Someone went first and did a lot of work that makes it easier to hike through the brush. We can cover in two hours what would take a day to do without the trail. The thing is no one can find the trail. When we leave the road, you say good-bye to civilization and start into the wilds of Alaska. The people I take out have to follow me as only I know the way.

The Christian life is very similar because people have gone before us, and we can reap the benefits. Maybe you are from a Christian family. That has a lot to do with your life. Others have to blaze the way as they are the first Christian in their family, so its new and takes blazing a path. All of us can point to several people who influenced us before we were Christians or in our early days as a new Christian. Many times I have heard someone who had lived as a non-Christian but finally came to the end of themselves. They give their life to Jesus and then remember their grandmother or grandfather, who are now gone, praying for them in the midst of their sinking life. Even in the midst of a sinful life, they knew someone was on the right trail, and they were off the trail and struggling in the thick brush.

But no matter what family you're from you still have to blaze a path for those following you. Each generation has to forge ahead in expanding the kingdom of God. Someone blazed a trail for you and you are reaping their work. You are also blazing a trail for those watching and following you. Stay on the trail and you will be able to offer hope and an easier way through life; you know the way.

* * * * *

As a Christian, what path are we blazing for others to follow? It's more than just going to church or singing songs. It's revealing a life of faith. It's revealing that we are following the ultimate pioneer who blazed a path for us to follow. Want to blaze a path for those to follow? Live a life of faith and follow Jesus. Stay on that path and don't get off into the brush.

It's amazing to think about the principle that we are leaving an example for others to follow, that our lives can be an example. Everyone has a ministry, and this is the ministry of being an example walking a path that others will follow.

Robert E. Lee once related an incident in which he was walking in the snow at Arlington. Lee's oldest son, Custis, was with him, and he noticed that the boy was lagging behind. As Lee turned to look for his son, he noticed the young boy was carefully stepping in his father's deep footprints in the snow. In later telling of the incident,

Lee said, "When I saw this, I said to myself, 'It behooves me to walk very straight, when this fellow is already following in my tracks.'"

"Follow my example, as I follow the example of Christ." (Corinthians 11:1 (NIV)

Don't lose heart as you follow Jesus's example because He made the trail for all of us to follow. You are leading others by your example.

Lesson on Fishing

To catch fish, you have to go where they are.

Seems like fishing and me don't get along. But there are a few things I have learned about fishing, especially from my time commercial fishing in Bristol Bay Alaska, in the early summer of 1982.

I learned that if you're going to fish, you have to go where the fish are. Secondly, you have to use bait that the fish like, and thirdly, it's always up to the fish to want your bait.

When commercial fishing you quickly learn that your whole life focuses on finding where the fish are and catching them. Hundreds of fishing boats full of hundreds of people flock to Bristol Bay for a few months of the year and are there for one reason and one reason only—to catch salmon. Fishermen want to catch fish as fast as possible, catch as many as possible, and never stop until the fish are gone or the season ends. The salmon are on their way up the endless rivers of Alaska to spawn and there is only a short window for fishing.

The Incredible Life of an Alaska Salmon

Alaska salmon have a most interesting life cycle. They have a life that takes them from the rivers and streams of Alaska's wilderness to the open seas of the Pacific Ocean and to return again. In fact, they return to the very place they were born. Incredibly, they find their way back from the vast expanse of the Pacific Ocean to the very spot they were hatched. Not to mention that they swim from freshwater to saltwater and back again.

Starting out as small eggs in a stream bed, they hatch and begin their journey downstream toward the ocean. They spend a couple of years in the streams and rivers growing into smolts. At the mouth of the streams and rivers, the smolts school together and get ready for their trip to the ocean. During this time, their bodies change as they prepare to live in the saltwater of the ocean. The salmon then head out to sea and spend several years swimming in the Bering Sea and the Gulf of Alaska. After they mature, they swim back to their original stream or river. They must readapt to the freshwater as they return to their spawning grounds. Sometimes this means swimming up huge rivers with miles of rapids and even waterfalls they must get over. If they aren't eaten by the many bears that are now feasting on them for their winter fat, they get back to the stream they were hatched in and lay their eggs. After spawning, they generally die within a week, fertilizing the stream and creating a fertile environment for the new salmon that are about to hatch.

To catch fish, you have to find the fish.

The fishing boats are constantly listening to the chatter on the CB radio for boats giving reports of how their fishing is going, usually to their friends. The trick is to figure out the codes the skippers use that will let you know where the fish are or aren't. If a boat mistakenly says they found where the fish are, your area will quickly look like the line at the church's coffee bar in the lobby after a megachurch is out. If you have a partner in another boat who found the fish in another area, they will speak in code so as not to alert other boats. You don't want a hundred boats coming to your area if you have found the fish.

You see you have to work as hard when you're not catching fish as you are catching them so why not catch them and make money.

Bristol Bay is 250 miles long and 180 miles wide at its mouth. A number of rivers flow into the Bay Area. These rivers flowing into it are where the fish are heading to spawn. This is why it is such a rich fishery. As they return to these rivers and head up to their places of birth, fishermen are trying to catch them. Your time to catch them is short as they are on a mission to return, and once they are gone, they are gone. Now take hundreds of boats all around the same areas fishing for them who are also in a hurry to return to their home with as much money as possible. That makes for a hurried frantic search of hundreds of boats running around desperately trying to find the fish, get as many as possible, quickly as possible, and get back home. Bristol Bay is a large body of open water, and to move from one location to another takes hours in the boat. It is a highly regulated industry by the state fisheries, so you have to be aware of the regulations. For instance, you have to be registered in an area to fish in that particular area. To move to a new area you have to register in the new area and you have a forty-eight-hour wait until you can fish in the new area. One time, we heard that the fish had come to another area, so the captain registered his boat for that new area, and off we went to that area. It would take us six hours in a rough sea to get across the bay. Since we were experiencing a storm and couldn't fish anyway, the skipper decided to make the change. All I remember is one minute looking at the sky like I was in the space shuttle heading to space and then the next minute feeling like the boat was heading to China via a direct line through the middle of the earth. Down it would go, hitting the water like hitting concrete after each swell, I felt like a toy being tossed around by a puppy for six hours. But you have to go where the fish are.

If you're going to fish, you have to use the bait they will like.

It's always amazing to visit an outdoor store and see the thousands of spinners, flies, fish eggs, and other things to put on the end of a pole. People that I take into my wilderness bush cabin always ask me what kind of bait the fish in the lake like. These are grayling that are suited for the high Alaska lakes, which are iced over seven months of the year. Many like to fly fish, and I tell them which ever species of bugs have hatched out at that time are what the fish are eating. Water temperatures and the time of day factor into hungry fish too. In other words, it takes attentive observation and research to know which bait the fish will bite.

It's always up to the fish to bite or not.

In the end, you can do all your research, have the best bait, but it's up to the fish to bite or not. It is frustrating for many if the bait is not taken.

133

"Come, follow me," Jesus said, "and I will send you out to fish for people." (Matthew 4:19 NIV)

In ministry, you have to go where the people are.

When you get to a place to "fish," look to see where the people are already gathered. I am not talking about finding them in another church body. When we first moved to Talkeetna, Alaska, in 1996, my young son was eleven. I noticed the small community had a lot of kids that played softball, so I started helping out with that and made lots of relationships. I found out quickly that the men like to get together on snow machine trips. I bought one and went with them. There are always groups gathered. Look and observe and go to that group instead of starting a new one. There will be time for your ideas, but you need to build relationships first. It's about going where the people are and building relationships so that they will trust you. It's a long lonely process to expect them to come to you. I have seen many eager people move to this area and start their ministry and expect the people to come to them. They last usually about one year and leave. Listen to the chatter and go where the fish are. When arriving to a new area, build relationships first. That is your ministry.

Your methods have to attract people.

If you move to a small community in Alaska, you better know the culture and what they do. If you want to reach the men, you better get active in what they do. If you want to reach families, see where they are gathering. If they love the community school team sports, then go to the games. Then you can decide on how to minister to the groups. I started a volleyball event for the youth group, and they all started coming because they love to play volleyball. The town used to do an event called "Moose Dropping" festival which had a parade event. We had the idea to make a float with the youth and it won first place for the most innovative!

In deciding which bait to use I have seen many use facts, research, and sermons that are supposed to attract many, but never substitute a pulpit ministry for relationships. In other words, using teaching only would be a rationalistic approach to ministry rather than a relational one. Even with the best explanations in an eight-week series on Calvinism and Arminianism, the gulf between the people and the fisherman grows more and more. Why? The bait may be correct, but the methods that are being used for that particular group are not building relationships. Jesus spent three years with His disciples, and most of it was outside the "classroom." It was doing life together and out in the "fields."

Ultimately the people decide.

It's always up to the people to decide whether they accept the methods being used. Remember people vote two ways, with their pocketbook and with their feet!

The job of a Christian leader is to develop people. It's about relationships, about discipleship, about developing people's body, soul, and spirit. People are not there to be part of your numbers. They are there to be part of your life so you can be part of theirs.

Married and partners in adventure since
1973 Mike and Molly Sloan

ABOUT THE AUTHOR

I grew up north of Seattle and became an early avid outdoor enthusiast. In high school, I started climbing mountains in the Cascades. In 1971, I was invited to join an expedition to climb Alaska's Mount McKinley (now Denali), which is the tallest mountain in North America from the little climb north side. Upon returning from the expedition and working at a climbing store, I met Molly, and we were married in 1973. We moved into a small mountain community called Green Water, Washington, and built our first log cabin. I worked in the woods logging and, in the winters worked, on the avalanche patrol at Crystal Mountain ski area. We moved to Eastern Washington and built our second log house. In 1982, At thirty years old, I got a job on a fishing boat in Alaska and, while on that trip, became a Christian, and my life changed. We received a call to missions and went to Bible school at Prairie Bible College in Alberta, Canada. After graduation, we went to Nepal and lived in a remote village in western Nepal for almost four years doing community development work as missionaries. When we returned from Nepal, I went to Wheaton College graduate school to receive a master's in education. Then we started pastoring, and I began developing a philosophy of ministry that used the outdoors for developing youth and families. We moved to Alaska in 1996 to pastor and planted a church in Talkeetna, Alaska, where we still live. In 2018, my son and I finished a twelve-year father-son project of climbing all the high points of all fifty states. I still travel to Nepal and recently completed the one-thousand-mile Great Himalaya trail that traverses Nepal from east to west. We have three children and six grandchildren. We have been in ministry since 1982, and I am still guiding wilderness trips in Alaska into my wilderness cabin next to Denali National Park.